EXTRACTS FROM LETTERS AND NOTES

WRITTEN

DURING THE SIEGE OF DELHI IN 1857

BY
GENERAL SIR CHARLES REID, G.C.B.

The Naval & Military Press Ltd
published in association with
FIREPOWER
The Royal Artillery Museum
Woolwich

Published by
The Naval & Military Press Ltd
Unit 10 Ridgewood Industrial Park,
Uckfield, East Sussex,
TN22 5QE England
Tel: +44 (0) 1825 749494
Fax: +44 (0) 1825 765701
www.naval-military-press.com

in association with

FIREPOWER
The Royal Artillery Museum, Woolwich
www.firepower.org.uk

In reprinting in facsimile from the original, any imperfections are inevitably reproduced and the quality may fall short of modern type and cartographic standards.

HINDOO RAO'S HOUSE, DELHI, 1857.

EXTRACTS

FROM

LETTERS AND NOTES WRITTEN DURING THE SIEGE OF DELHI IN 1857,

BY

GENERAL SIR CHARLES REID, G.C.B.

ABOUT noon, on the 14th May, 1857, I received an express from Head-Quarters, directing me to march with my regiment, the Sirmoor Battalion, to Meerut, to aid the Europeans at that station in suppressing the mutiny of the native troops. My orders were issued immediately, and four hours after receipt of the Commander-in-Chief's order the regiment was on the move. Waiting for carriage for the conveyance of tents and baggage was out of the question, so we marched out of Deyrah with just what we carried on our backs : sixty rounds of ammunition in pouch, and two elephant loads of spare ammunition. I had previously heard from Major (now Colonel) Baird Smith at "Roorkee," that in the event of my being ordered to Meerut, he would suggest my taking the canal route, and that he would have fifty boats ready for me. As Meerut was ten long marches, which at the season of the year I could not have done in less than four or five days, and at the end of which my men would have been quite exhausted and unfit for hard work, I at once determined on taking the "Canal route," thinking I should reach Meerut in three days from the time of leaving Deyrah, and with the advantage of having my men perfectly fresh, and ready for work on landing. I accordingly marched to "Roorkee," making "Kheree" (twenty-eight miles) my first march, ten miles of which was over the stony "Mohun pass." At "Kheree," on the morning of 15th May, I heard from Baird Smith of the mutiny of the sappers at Meerut, and the probability of an outbreak amongst the sappers left at "Roorkee." Up to that time they had not openly broken out, although they had refused to obey orders. He begged of me to hasten on, and that in the meantime he would get all the ladies and Europeans into the workshops which could be defended. I marched immediately after receipt of this communication, and early on the morning of the 16th, after a long and tedious march, reached "Roorkee." When within three miles of the place, I received a note from Baird Smith begging of me not to march on farther in the direction of the station of "Roorkee," as my movements were watched by the sappers, and that ere I could reach the place the mischief would have been done; that up to that time the sappers were quiet, but that their suspicions were raised by my movements, and he thought it best to show them they were still trusted, and that, if I moved off quietly in the direction of where my boats were, nothing would be thought of the appearance of the Goorkahs at "Roorkee." He was right beyond doubt, and his good judgment and forethought may have been—indeed I feel pretty sure was—the means of saving the place, and lives of the ladies and children. I deemed it necessary to make it appear that I had lost my way in the dark, and that I did not intend to go to the "Roorkee" station, but to the canal bridge, where my boats were ready for me. I accordingly told the messenger who brought the note to get me a guide from the nearest village to take me to the canal. My move to the bridge instead of the direction of the station of "Roorkee" was of course communicated to the sappers, and happily all went well. Owing to the great exertions of Baird Smith, I found forty-five boats all ready for me, but ere we stepped on board it was necessary to give my men time to get something to eat. Whilst thus employed, I saw several of the sappers, who had come from "Roorkee" to see what we were about, moving backwards and forwards amongst my men, and talking in an earnest manner to them ; some of them passed close to me with an insolent look and an air of defiance. I called one or two of them back, after they had swaggered past me, and asked them whether it was not customary to salute an officer in uniform. After looking at one another, they saluted me, and said "they had forgotten to do so." Presently I saw a large number of them talking to my Goorkahs. I took no notice at the time, but as soon as they moved on I called up a couple of my men and asked them what the sappers had said to them. One little fellow replied, "They wanted to know if we were going over to Meerut to eat the 'Otta,' sent up especially for the Goorkahs by the Governor-General; that the 'otta'-flour at Meerut was nothing but ground bullocks' bones!" "And what was your reply?" "I said the regiment was going wherever it was ordered—we obey the bugle call." About 9 o'clock we embarked, and away we went down the Great Ganges Canal at the rate of about five miles an hour; but I found it necessary to sound the halt every now and then to enable the boats to close up—a necessary precaution, as the whole country was up in arms against us. About sunset, as we were getting the boats through one of the locks, the line of skirmishers, which I had out on the right bank, reported a party of " red-coats." These turned out to be a party of the 29th N.I., who had just been relieved from Treasury duty at Saharunpore.

I had no reason to suppose that they had mutinied, or that the regiment was in any way disaffected, but immediately they saw my men the party halted, and commenced loading their muskets. This looked suspicious, so I at once ordered the leading company to jump out of their boats and to load. Before they could get out, a native officer of the party of the 29th Native Infantry come forward and said he wished to speak to me. I went forward and found him most respectful in his manner. He told me he and his party had just been relieved from duty at Saharunpore, and that they were on their way to

"Mooradabad," to join the head-quarters of the regiment. I remarked that they had a good deal of baggage with them, seeing some eight or ten camels laden, which I made sure was all "loot" (plunder). I asked him what made his men load, to which he replied that they had got frightened on seeing the regiment. "Well," I said, " I hope you and your regiment are all right; bring up your men, and proceed along the road, and as you pass me 'carry arms.'" I then went back to the regiment, and told the men to get into their boats again, being anxious to show the men of the 29th Native Infantry that I trusted them, and considered they and their regiment were loyal. The native officer did what he could, but the men evidently thought I was laying a trap for them, and all of a sudden they took to their heels. Feeling sure that what they did was from sheer fright, I did not pursue them, nor did I allow a shot to be fired. Two days after I heard that the regiment was loyal, and had put down one or two disturbances in the Mooradabad district. As we could not proceed in our boats at night, owing to the falls of the canal, and the difficulty even during the day of getting into the lock channels, I disembarked for the night, and, after taking our dinner, we lay down to rest on the canal bank.

The next day, the 17th May, I found great difficulty in keeping my boats together, and did not make so much progress as I thought I should have done. About noon we came across a number of the sappers who had mutinied at Meerut, but they would not allow my skirmishers to get near them. The whole country being up in arms against us, I had the greatest difficulty in procuring supplies from the villages, and in many cases at the bayonet point. Again we made our bed on the canal bank, but sleeping was out of the question, owing to the uproar on all sides. The "Goojurs" were of course at their dear old game of plundering, and the firing and shouting that went on around, coupled with the great heat, rendered it impossible to get anything like a wink of sleep. A number of officers who were on leave at Mussoorie, and who had been ordered down to join their regiments, overtook me on the road to "Roorkee," so that we had a very jolly party, and rather a noisy one too, but as there was tumult on all sides it did not much signify.

On the 18th May, at 5 P.M., I reached "Nanoo," opposite the station of Meerut. I was met by an officer of the Canal Department, who I was glad to see at his post, though the whole of his establishment had deserted him. He gave me a letter from General Hewitt, commanding Meerut Division, the purport of which was to push on as fast as I could to "Boolundshur," and if possible to save the treasure which a company of the 9th N.I. had charge of. The 9th Regiment, he mentioned, was still loyal, but he had reasons to think that they would not remain so long. Two hundred of the Gwalior Cavalry were to join me at "Boolundshur," and the treasure, if I thought it advisable, might be sent under escort of the cavalry to Meerut. It was too late to proceed further that night, so 1 took up my ground on the left bank of the canal for the night. The next morning, the 19th May, two or three of my native officers came up and reported that one of the sappers from Meerut (out of the few who remained when the regiment mutinied) had been with the regiment during the whole night, and had been telling the men that they were going to Meerut, and on arrival that the regiment would be placed in the " Dum-Dummer," with the 60th Rifles on one side, and the artillery on the other, and that they would be cut to pieces ! I told them I was pleased to hear from them all that went on, and that their conduct was very praiseworthy in reporting all such matters. The regiment was drawn up at the time in line preparatory to embarking, but the men had not the slightest idea whether they were going to Meerut or not. I gave the order " Pass by files to the rear, and jump into your boats." The canal officer, Mr. Parker, told me that he thought we should find the canal locks destroyed, and that we should experience great difficulty in getting through the lock channels. The people, he said, were all in open rebellion, and had refused to give him any assistance in the protection of the canal property at the different stations ; indeed, in many instances, they had been the first to plunder Government property, but that the sight of the regiment at the different " chokees " would have a wonderful effect, and he hoped that order would be restored. Mr. Parker was armed to the teeth—and well he might be, for he told me he had had to fly for his life on several occasions since the mutiny broke out at Meerut. As we passed down the canal crowds of natives were to be seen on the bridges, which we came to every three miles. All were armed, but after looking to see who we were, and what we were about, they moved off.

On the 20th we came to the "Bhola Locks," which we found completely destroyed, the whole of the working apparatus was gone, and we found we could not move the flood-gates. The station house was in ruins, and the whole of the Government property had been plundered. A search in the adjacent villages I immediately ordered, being determined to make a few examples of these gentlemen. I sent a company off in the first instance to search the village of "Bhola." The people all turned out armed, and, on being asked to give them up, they positively refused; and some advanced towards my men. The quartermaster-sergeant, whom I had sent with the company, and to whom I had given instructions, on seeing the men advance with their arms, ordered the leading section of the company to fire a volley. This at once settled the matter; down went the arms and off went the villagers. A search was then made, and eighteen prisoners taken, in whose houses Government property was found, including electric telegraph wire, &c.

Demi Official.

Extract of a letter addressed to the Quartermaster-General of the Army, dated "Bhola Locks," Ganges Canal, 21st May, 1857.

Here I am making the best of my way to "Boolundshur." I left Deyrah at 4 P.M. the 14th inst. (four hours after the receipt of your express, dated 12th inst.), reached "Kheree," twenty-eight miles, at daybreak on the 15th inst.; pushed on to Roorkee, arrived at daybreak on the 16th inst. Here I found boats ready for my regiment; embarked at 9 A.M., but did not reach "Nanoo" before 5 P.M. on the 18th. Great delay in getting the boats through the locks, and detained, owing to the difficulty in keeping the fleet of boats (forty-five in number) together, which was a necessary precaution, as I came across two or three parties of rebels, who would not, however, allow me to get near them. "Goojurs" plundering and burning villages in all directions. I received instructions when opposite Meerut to continue progress by canal to "Boolundshur," and, if possible, to save the treasure at that place.

I reached this place, "Bhola," yesterday, at 9 A.M.; found the whole of the working apparatus gone, and the locks very much injured; the flood-gate chains, ropes, &c., had all been plundered by the villagers on the canal banks. Most of the chains, iron bolts, &c., as also miles and miles of electric telegraph wire found in the village of "Bhola;" took eighteen prisoners, in whose houses Government property was found. Burnt the village. The prisoners will be tried this evening by a drumhead court-martial, and if found guilty I shall shoot them. My men were working hard at the locks all yesterday, and again to-day rigging up an apparatus for forcing the flood-gates open.* Fortunately I have two of the canal officers with me (Walker and Parker), and they are indefatigable in their exertions. We hope to get all the boats through the lock by to-morrow morning. The damage done at this lock alone is estimated at 30,000 rs. We fully expect to find the next lock in the same state.

The rebels have a small post at " Mooradnuggur," which I am not far from. I shall pay them a visit. They are also supposed to have two guns, and a small detachment at " Shadaree," on the left bank of the Jumna.

The Commander-in-Chief, I hear, is to be at Kurnaul to-day. Delhi I fancy he will reach about the 23rd inst. Waterfield, the Deputy Assistant Adjutant-General at Meerut, writes that I may have to move to " Ghazeeodeen-nuggur " on the Hindun to prevent the rebels escaping from Delhi into the Doab. All I require is *information*. Meerut people send me none; they appear to have lost their heads ! At this present moment I don't know how many regiments have mutinied. Send me intelligence on receipt of this.

My little fellows are in capital order, grinding their teeth again to get at the rebels.

May 22nd.—Thirteen out of the eighteen prisoners

---

* The body of a European woman was found in the lock—probably the wife of one of the sergeants employed on the canal.

were found guilty, and I had them shot last evening
by my men : five out of the thirteen were Brahmins.
I left copies of the Governor-General's order proclaiming martial law on the trees near the dead
bodies. This will have a good effect I think. I have
got all my boats through the lock, and push on at
once to "Boolundshur."

Please pay the messenger 50 rs., and send him
back with all the information you can give me.

C. R.

Ganges Canal, May 23rd.

I was proceeding with my fleet of boats in
column (three abreast), with two companies in extended order on either bank of the canal, when the
"alarm" was given by the leading skirmishers on
the right bank. I sounded the "halt" and made
arrangements for disembarking ; but before I could
do so my skirmishers became engaged. The rebels,
seeing I was prepared for them, made off after firing
a few shots. They were all villagers, no sepoys I
think amongst them. My men followed them until
they were recalled by bugle.

On the 24th of May, at daybreak, I landed my
regiment at one of the canal stations opposite Boolundshur, and marched into the place, which I found
completely destroyed. The treasure was gone ; the
company of the 9th N.I. having walked off with it
to Delhi three days before. The civilians had been
driven out, and had flown to Meerut, and there was
not a human being to be seen in what had been the
civil station of "Boolundshur." As I expected the

rebels to pay me a visit in force, I selected a good position, and set to work to entrench myself. Shortly after my arrival some of the native officials made their appearance. I directed them to send men round to the different villages, and to inform the people that martial law was in force; that I had already made a few examples, and intended to make a few more; that they had better produce the electric telegraph wire and posts which had been removed the whole way between Boolundshur and Meerut; and last, but not least, that a gallows was to be erected immediately in front of my entrenchments. It was amusing to see the look the native officials gave me. They saw, however, that I was in earnest, and before 12 o'clock the gallows was erected. Supplies were brought in, and a couple of tents were produced, which we were much in need of. I wrote off to the General at Meerut reporting my arrival, and requested him to send the civil officers back to their post as soon as possible. About an hour after my arrival my picquets reported that a body of cavalry was advancing. They turned out to be 400 of the Rampoor Horse, sent by the Nawab of Rampoor at the instigation of the Commissioner, Mr. Greathead. I saw at once by the look of these gentlemen that they were rather shaky. Their leader, an Afghan, refused to obey my orders, on which I ordered him out of the place, and told him the sooner he marched the better. He afterwards sent one of his officers to say that he begged forgiveness, and that he would do anything he was ordered; that I was his lord and master, &c. Being anxious to get rid of them, I ordered a couple of hundred to detach themselves along the Allyghur and Meerut roads, in order to keep the communication open. All was quiet by evening ; a large supply of provisions was brought in, and the natives were civil. If we could only have got a carriage, we might have taken a drive on the course by way of restoring confidence! Mr. Sapte, the collector and magistrate, and his assistant arrived the next day. As martial law was in force, he of course asked my permission to resume his functions. The first question he asked was, "Might he collect revenue ? " " Oh, yes," I replied ; " and make the rascals pay double for all the mischief they have done." His zillah seal, the only thing that could be found near his "Kutchery," had been brought to me. This I gave up, and he and his assistant resumed their functions.

Demi Official.

Camp Boolundshur,

Urgent. *May 27th, 1857.*

To the Deputy Assistant Adjutant-General, Meerut.

All quiet here. No dâk in as yet from Meerut. I have, I think, opened the communication. I have twenty Sawors at Haúper, and the same number at "Gowloutee." A number of the Irregular Cavalry men who were on furlough in this neighbourhood have joined me, and I am making use of them. I require an officer to command them ; have not heard anything of the force assembling at "Hatrass." I have written to the officer commanding.

I have sent off a party of the Rampoor Horse to keep open the communication between this and Allyghur.

I searched the village of "Chandpore" this morning; found miles of E.T. wire and posts, buggies, horses, and other property belonging to the civil authorities of this place, burnt the village, took six prisoners in whose houses Government property was found: just about to try them by drumhead courtmartial; if convicted, I shall hang them. Arms taken in heaps; have not heard as yet what the Rampoor Horse have done at "Dadree" and "Secundrabad;" last letter received from you dated 25th, 1.30 P.M. Send me information regarding the movements of the Commander-in-Chief, and all you can collect anent the mutineers. I have no idea how many Regiments have mutinied. I require more European officers— smart fellows; send five or six. There must be any number of officers at Meerut whose Regiments have mutinied. Send Lieut. Ross of the 9th N.I., please. He commanded the detachment here, and knows the country round about Boolundshur.—C. R.

To the Deputy Assistant Adjutant-General, Meerut, dated Boolundshur, 28th May, 1857.
 Urgent.

MY DEAR WATERFIELD,—All quiet, and confidence restored. Hung the head man of the village of

"Chandpore," and two other rascals, in whose houses Government property was found. Have opened communication with Meerut, I hope also with Allyghur. The Goojurs said to be in force at " Dadree " and " Kuthara "—" Bishun Sing " their Commander-in-Chief ! ! The " Rampoor Horse " not to be trusted. I'm watching them. E.T. wire I hope to have repaired in a day or two. I require wire and posts. Send from Meerut, please. Write often and let me know what letters you receive from me, dates, &c. My Goorkahs in high spirits, and eager for action. I am in communication with Mr. Harvey and Mr. Vansittart at Agra. I have forwarded several communications from the Governor General to the Lieutenant Governor, also to Punjaub Government. I hope they have reached? Affairs below are no better than in the N.W. Troops are expected in Calcutta shortly! They have somewhat lost their heads in Calcutta! Some of the despatches which I have forwarded were torn up, but I took copies of them after I had put them together.—C. R.

Demi Official.

Urgent.   *Boolundshur, 29th May,* 1857.

MY DEAR WATERFIELD,—The " Rampoor Horse " mutinied last evening. Have sent them to the right about. I was just about to attack them in their camp, when I was informed they had taken to their heels ; they have gone to Delhi, I imagine—a good riddance ; I could have done more in this district had it not been for them—I had to watch them from the first. Why were they ever sent here ? A great mistake. They were in hopes of arriving here in time to walk off with the treasure, but the company of the 9th N.I. were too sharp for that, and took it to Delhi three days before I arrived.

C. R.

Urgent.   *Boolundshur,* 30*th May,* 1857.

MY DEAR WATERFIELD,—I have made over the Irregular Cavalry to Captain Tyrwhitt, a smart officer.

Brigadier Wilson writes me that he is hard up for troops on the Hindun. He has only one wing of a regiment of Infantry. He tells me that the Commander-in-Chief had ordered that I should take up a position on the Hindun, with my own regiment, 400 Cavalry, and four Horse-Artillery guns. This order has not as yet reached me; but as Brigadier Wilson appears most anxious that I should join him at once, I think I had better do so. He leaves the matter to my own discretion. All is quiet here, and Tyrwhitt can keep open the communication; I shall, therefore, march this evening for Brigadier Wilson's camp.

I do this on my own responsibility. I hope the General will approve : I am only anticipating the Commander-in-Chief's order, and, by so doing, I may be of service to Brigadier Wilson, who evidently thinks he is not strong enough for the mutineers at Delhi, who will attack him to a certainty.

I have *no* tents, and only 60 rounds of ammunition in pouch and two elephant loads of spare ammunition. Could not get carriage at Deyrah. Please send to the Hindun as soon as possible. The heat frightful. I left two companies of Goorkahs at Deyrah for protection of ladies and children. I armed the Line boys. Had some spare arms fortunately in store.—C.R.

Left Boolundshur at 6 P.M. on the 30th May; heat frightful. We marched twenty-seven miles along the left bank of the canal; men dead beat; hot wind blowing all night. Bivouacked under a few thin baubul trees at 11 A.M. on the 31st. Resumed march at sunset, and after marching the whole night and until 10 A.M. on the 1st June, I at length reached Brigadier Wilson's camp. I found the whole country under water, in consequence of the damage done by the rebels to the canal bunds and escape channels. I had the greatest difficulty in getting along; my little men at times almost swimming; the hot sun overhead, and the glare from the water was something fearful. I found Brigadier Wilson as I expected, in rather an awkward predicament. He had a fight on the 30th, and another on the 31st. He had taken five guns in his first fight, but in his second he had had great difficulty in driving the rebels back, and had not succeeded in taking any of their guns. His troops had behaved most nobly, but they were knocked down by the sun, and were completely exhausted; so much so that the Brigadier quite dreaded another attack, which he was evidently expecting. He was rejoiced at my having joined him so soon; he had not received any of my notes, and was taken quite by surprise. I was of course taken for an enemy advancing in his rear. The whole force turned out and cheered the regiment into camp ; but my poor little fellows were so dead beat they could not return the hearty cheers with which they were welcomed. " Get something to eat sharp," said the Brigadier, " as we may have to turn out." Exhausted as my men were, I certainly was not anxious for a fight, and was thankful the mutineers left us alone that day. On the 2nd June I was ordered by the Brigadier to take my own regiment and two companies of the 60th Royal Rifles, and attack a village occupied by the enemy on our left front. I made my arrangements, and approached with the Rifles in extended order, and my own regiment in support ; but I had not gone far before I discovered that the village had been vacated. I had to destroy the place ; so after knocking the walls of the houses down, which I soon effected by the aid of a dozen elephants, I set fire to the grass roofs. The heat of the sun was fearful, to which was added the heat of the fire, and the hot wind which came in fiery blasts through the high flames can be better imagined than described. No blasts of a furnace could have been hotter. Yet all worked cheerfully, and my work was over in three hours.

On the 3rd June we got tents for the regiment from Meerut, which we were much in need of, having been without them since leaving Deyrah. The men, being accustomed to a cold climate, feel the heat just as much as Europeans, but they look well and jolly. We thought we should have been attacked to-day, but we remained unmolested. Got ammunition all safe from Meerut this afternoon. Four officers joined me and we established a mess. Left Ghazeeodeen Nuggur at 4 P.M. on the 4th June, to join the Commander-in-Chief's camp at Allipore. I have command of the rear guard—two squadrons of the Carabineers, four Horse Artillery guns, and my own regiment. Great delay in getting the camels and carts over the Hindun bridge. Got all over by twelve o'clock at night. Bridge destroyed by our engineers. Marched all night. Halts every half-hour to admit of the baggage closing up. Did not reach the camp until 4.30 P.M. on the 5th June. Men under arms and marching for twenty-four and a half hours! Encamped at "Kakree" for two hours and a half only. Resumed march, and reached the bridge of boats at Bagput at daybreak on the 6th June. Left Bagput at 2 A.M., and reached Allipore on the 7th, about 9 A.M. Here we joined the force under Sir H. Barnard. Marched into the camp, but not a cheer for us; on the contrary, all looked upon the Goorkahs with an eye of suspicion, which was very discouraging, after what my little fellows had already done.* I was not questioned myself, but several asked my officers whether they thought the Goorkahs were to be trusted; when I was told of this, I said, "Time will

* So suspicious was the General of the Goorkahs that he actually had a camp pitched for us on the extreme left of the line, with the Artillery close to us ready to *pound* us if we misbehaved. I could not make out why they had so *kindly* pitched tents for us, but learnt afterwards all about it.

show." " Shooting Brahmins," I said, " was a pretty good test." I must not forget to mention that two out of the three men I hanged at Boolundshur were Brahmins, and, strange to say, both of their ropes broke. No sooner had their feet touched the ground than I ordered (I had a company drawn up in front of the gallows) " Two files to the front—quick march —ready—present!" The men fired just as if they had been firing at a target on parade. Over went the two Brahmins, dead. My strict discipline has told well : I have merely to give an order and am obeyed immediately. We attack the mutineers at " Budlee-ke-Serai " to-morrow morning.

Extracts from Letters and Notes written from the Main Picquet, Hindôo Rao's House.

Hindôo Rao's House, June 8th, 1857.—" Left Allipore at 1 A.M.; found the enemy in force in a very strong position about seven miles from Delhi, ' Budle-ke-Serai.' After about two hours' fighting we drove them from their position, and pursued them until they got behind the strong walls of Delhi. Captured thirteen guns, and gave them a sound good thrashing. About 1 P.M. we reached the Ridge, when I was directed by General Barnard to occupy 'Hindôo Rao's House,' which is within twelve hundred yards of the 'Moree Bastion.' Had just made ourselves comfortable, when the 'alarm' was sounded. In ten minutes the mutineers were seen coming up towards Hindôo Rao's House in force. I went out with my own regiment, two companies of Rifles, and two guns of Scott's Battery, and drove them back into the city. This, however, was not accomplished till 5 P.M., so that we were under arms for sixteen hours. Heat fearful; my little fellows behaved splendidly, and were cheered by every European Regiment. It was the only *Native* Regiment with force, and I may say every eye was upon it. The General was anxious to see what the *Goorkahs* could do, and if we were to be *trusted!* They had (because it was a *Native* Regiment) *doubts* about us, but I think they are now satisfied." I wanted to turn the captured heavy guns on the enemy, but we had *no shot* for them! They soon made us a present of a few, and we sent them back again.

"Hindôo Rao's House" was the key of the position we had taken up before Delhi, and which the enemy were not long in discovering; they tried their utmost to drive me out of it the first day, and it became ever after the object of almost every attack. I felt highly honoured in being selected for the command of this post, and expressed my thanks to the General, who afterwards was pleased to entrust me with the command of all the posts on the right of the Ridge, including the "Main Picquet," "Observatory," "Sammy House," "Crow's Nest," and "Subzeemundy," and which I had the good fortune to hold till the 14th September, 1857.

On the 8th June, I had only my own regiment (never more than 490 strong, including all grades) two companies of the 60th Royal Rifles, and two light guns.*

About noon on the 9th June, I was reinforced by the gallant Corps of Guides, which arrived in camp a few hours before they were sent up to me, after making the most wonderful march down from the Punjab. They were all ready, they told me, for work, and by 2 P.M. they were hotly engaged, and I saw at once what an acquisition they were to my small force. The corps is composed chiefly of Seikhs and Punjabees, and they have a company of Goorkahs 100 strong. Most of the latter tribe were enlisted by me for the regiment at Petoraghur in 1852, but at the end of the siege they had not more than 15 or 20 left.

Whenever I sounded the "alarm," which indicated an attack upon my own position, the General sent me up from camp two more companies of the 60th Royal Rifles as a "support." My own regiment and one company of the Rifles occupied the House, and one company of the Rifles the "Observatory," where a battery for three heavy guns was constructed on the night of the 9th, to reply to the "Cashmere Bastion." The centre battery for three 18-pounders was close to the house, and the guns were all laid for the "Moree Bastion." The Guides I located in and behind the outhouses. The two companies of the 60th Royal Rifles were at first relieved daily; but this I found objectionable, as it often so happened

---

* It will be seen that my Letters and Notes are very brief, but it could not be otherwise, as I had no time for *composition*.

that I was attacked just at the time the relief took place, and after I had made my disposition for the defence of the right flank. I accordingly made arrangements with the General for their relief once a week, which pleased the officers, and men too. I longed to have the whole corps under my command, but this could not be. My time, when we were not fighting, was fully occupied in watching the movements of the enemy, which will I trust be sufficient excuse for the brief account given of each action in the following extracts. The few lines were always written under great difficulties, for it must be borne in mind that we were under the fire of the enemy's heavy bastions morning, noon and night from first to last.

June 9th.—" We got two heavy guns in position this morning, when we were able to reply to the ' Moree Bastion.' Two more guns opened at 1 P.M. At 2 P.M. we were again attacked ; the whole of the Guide Infantry, which arrived to-day, were sent up to me to strengthen the Picquet, and a support of 200 of the 60th Rifles. We met the scoundrels coming up the road. I threw out skirmishers on the right and left, and allowed them to approach. We were fighting until 4 P.M., when the enemy retreated with heavy loss. A fine large verandah on the east side of Hindôo Rao's House was knocked to pieces during the day ; the practice was first-rate from the ' Moree,' and the 24-pounder shot soon battered it down."

June 10th.—" Another engagement this afternoon ; the mutineers came out in force with guns and

Cavalry. I turned out the 'Main Picquet,' 7 companies of my own regiment, 2 companies of Rifles, 2 guns of Major Scott's Battery, and 150 of the Guide Infantry. I took up a good position and waited until our friends came close up: the Guides I extended in skirmishing order in front, the Rifles extended on my left flank; guns in the centre, supported by 7 companies of my own regiment. The skirmishers soon became engaged. The enemy opened with their 9-pounder guns on my right, and it became necessary to strengthen the line of skirmishers, which I did by throwing forward a company of Goorkahs in continuation of the first line. Whilst my men were advancing, the mutineers called out, 'Come on, Goorkahs; we won't fire upon *you*—we expect you to join us.' 'Oh, yes,' was the reply, 'we are coming.' They closed upon their centre, and when within 20 paces they gave the mutineers a well-directed volley, killing some 30 or 40 of the scoundrels. The scrimmage lasted until 7.30 P.M., when the enemy thought they had had enough of it, and withdrew. My loss this evening in my own regiment 3 killed and 10 wounded; the Guides, 3 killed and 3 wounded; 3 horses killed in Scott's Battery, and 3 wounded. The Rifles did not lose a man; I kept them as much under cover as possible. We were out at 4 P.M. and did not get back to the Main Picquet (Hindôo Rao's House) until near nightfall. Poor Quintin Battye was killed on the evening of the 9th; a sad loss. He was a first-rate soldier."

June 11*th*.—" A day of comparative rest: no enemy

appeared. The 'Moree,' 'Cashmere,' 'Burn,' and
'River' Bastions kept up a constant fire upon the
Picquet, and the house suffered a good deal. The
ammunition for the Centre and Left Batteries was
stowed away in the right wing of Hindôo Rao's House.
This we found rather a difficult matter under the
heavy fire from the enemy's bastions, which was kept
up the whole day. Earth was thrown over the roof,
but I cannot say I ever thought the magazine very
secure. The House was, moreover, in a direct line
of fire, and every shot from the 'Moree' Bastion that
missed the Centre Battery struck the House."

June 12*th*.—" I was attacked this morning. The
mutineers were driven back in a very short space
of time with a loss to them of about 200. About
80 or 90 of the 4th Irregular Cavalry went over
to the enemy during the scrimmage. They passed
close to me, but little did I think they were going
to join the mutineers. They went to the front just
as if they were going to charge, but no sooner had
they closed than to my horror I saw them mix
up with the enemy, and walk off with them.
Immediately I saw this I ordered the guns to open
upon them, but the wretches were too far off, and I
don't think more than half a dozen of them were
killed. The enemy mounting more guns in the
'Moree' and 'Burn' Bastions. We are not likely
to take Delhi just at *present!* It is all we can do to
hold our own, and our guns cannot keep down the
fire from their batteries. We have ten heavy guns
at this picquet in constant play; the heat is some-

thing fearful, but the troops, thank God, are healthy."

June 13*th*.—" We heard this morning that two new regiments of mutineers had arrived in the city ; that they were being armed, and would attack us at 4 P.M. Sure enough on they came, making the best of their way for this position. I was all ready for them, and allowed them to come up within twenty paces, when I opened with grape and musketry on all sides. I charged them with a couple of companies (one the 60th Rifles and one of my own) over the hill. My loss 3 killed and 11 wounded ; 3 right arms amputated. The Guides 2 killed and 9 wounded, including Lieutenant Kennedy severely wounded, and who was a great loss to the Guides. No return of the loss in the Rifles as yet. The action was not over until 7.30 P.M. The 60th N.I. was one of the regiments that attacked us. They marched up the Grand Trunk Road in columns of sections right in front, and led the attack, headed by the Sirdar Bahadoor of the regiment, who made himself very conspicuous, calling out to his men to keep distance, as he intended to wheel to his left. They fought most desperately. The Sirdar Bahadoor of the 60th was killed by my orderly Lall Sing. I took the ribbon of India from his breast. The mutineers were about 5,000 strong, Infantry and Cavalry. Immediately I go out to attack, or rather to resist their attacks, my men are brought under the fire of their heavy guns from the walls of Delhi. The fire of the ' Moree,' ' Cashmere,' and ' Burn ' Bastions is something fearful, and the wonder is any one escapes. The present strength of the 'Main Picquet' is 4 companies 60th Rifles, the Sirmoors about 380 strong, 300 Guide Infantry, and 3 light guns, 7 heavy guns in battery, and two mortars, but these give us no assistance when we are attacked. They are all laid for the Moree Bastion, which has not suffered in the least, and we have done their defences no harm whatever. We have only one 24-pounder, which we took from the mutineers on the 8th; we had no *shot* for it, but the enemy soon made us a *present* of a few. We expect another attack to-morrow. I only wish the rascals would give us time to put on a clean shirt; I have not had one on for three days, which is by no means pleasant in such weather as this. Obliged to be on the alert morning, noon, and night."

It had been arranged that the city should be carried by a *coup-de-main*, and it was to have come off an hour or so before daybreak on the 13th June; but owing to the Brigadier of the day having declined to allow his picquets on the left to be withdrawn without a written order from the General (in which matter he was perfectly justified), the scheme was for that night abandoned. I cannot say I ever thought we should have succeeded; indeed am pretty confident it would have been a complete failure. The only chance of success would have been a surprise; but I never could allow that "Pandy" was so much off his guard as others made out. If secrecy had been preserved until we got close up to the gates, it is as much as could have been expected. Say we had so far succeeded : it often so happens that there is delay in proceeding farther ; either the men carrying the powder-bags are shot down, or the fuses won't light readily, or the explosion is not what was anticipated. Any of these mishaps with the handful of men of which the assailing columns were composed, with *no* reserve to fall back upon in case of disaster, would, in my humble opinion, have ended in defeat. The risk was a fearful one—the loss of India was in the balance.

My part of the affair was to have marched down the Grand Trunk Road with my own regiment, not 400 strong, accompanied by two engineer officers (Lieutenants Geneste and Fulford) and 20 Sappers ; blow open the " Lahore Gate," and make the best of my way down the " Chandnee Choke," and take up a position near the " Kotwallee," until joined by the other attacking column. To have accomplished this I should have had to pass close to the left and flank faces of the " Burn Bastion," which at that time mounted four, if not five, 18 and 24 pounders, besides being exposed to the fire from the loopholes. Had I succeeded in getting into the city with my 400 Goorkahs, I venture to say not one of them would ever have reached the " Kotwallee " in the " Chandnee Choke." We know what street fighting is, and I know pretty well what amount of grape from heavy guns men can stand. I may be wrong, but my own impression is, I could not, under any circumstances, have succeeded with *my* column, whatever the other might have done. However, I had merely to obey the written orders I received from General Barnard. I marched down to the "General's Mound" at 1.30 A.M.; but after waiting for the Sappers, powder-bags, &c., for about a quarter of an hour, up rode the Quartermaster-General of the Army, saying that the order had been countermanded, and begging of me to get back again to "Hindôo Rao's House" as quickly as possible.

The 60th Rifles had been ordered down as a covering or "firing party;" but the object of this I could never discover; there was no breach to keep clear, and little harm, I imagine, would have been done, by firing at the enemy behind the thick walls of Delhi. Twenty picked riflemen for each column would have sufficed for the purpose of watching the loopholes above, and on either side the gates, whilst the powder-bags were being placed. But it would appear that a general attack on loopholes was intended!

The only chance that men have of firing into loopholes is by getting close up to them. The closer you are the less you are exposed to the *direct* fire from other loopholes. But how the 60th Rifles were to get close up to the walls of Delhi, without jumping the ditch, and being exposed to the flank fire of the heavy bastions, I never could make out. The very men who would have been all, everything, with the attacking columns were thus disposed of, but, thank God! the attack never took place. Hodson and a few others were very sanguine of the success of the *coup-de-main*, but it was, in my humble opinion, a mad idea. The enemy I always found on the alert at night. This I put to the test more than once, but my Goorkahs invariably returned with a shake of the head; "'Burra Hosia' wide awake!" said they, with a broad grin.

When our reinforcements arrived, it was again proposed that the city should be taken by a *coup-de-main*. One column was to effect an entrance by blowing in the iron grating of the canal near the Cabul Gate; another to enter the Cashmere Gate, and a third to escalade the Cashmere Bastion; but, owing to my having been attacked on the night of the 2nd July, it was again abandoned. My regiment was to have been attached to the first assaulting column, which must have failed as it turned out afterwards, the canal grating being commanded by the flank fire of the "Moree Bastion," and one heavy gun pointed down the dry bed of the canal, along which our advance would have been made! The three columns and reserve would not have mustered more than 3,000 men (if so many), so it does not seem matter of regret that I was attacked by the enemy that night, instead of our attacking them behind their strong defences! At this time the mutineers mustered strong, having been joined two days previously by the Bareilly Brigade, consisting of No. 15 Horse Battery (two 6-pounder guns) from Shahjehanpore, the 8th Irregular Cavalry, 18th, 28th, 29th, and 68th Native Infantry; rather a formidable reinforcement.

June 14th.—"A day of rest, *Sunday*, very kind of them. Heavy batteries at work; the house is strong, but if they keep up this heavy fire it cannot stand long. My Goorkahs at work blocking up the windows of the house with sandbags."

June 15th.—" I was attacked this morning in great force, some 6,000 Infantry and Cavalry. The rascals had the impudence to bring out a couple of 9-pounders. I made all my arrangements for defence of the Picquets, and then went out with all available troops to attack the enemy as they came over the hill. I had six companies of my own regiment, and two guns of Scott's Battery ; I accordingly took up a position and waited for the mutineers to advance. On they came and placed a green standard on the hill, within a hundred paces of me! This was more than I could stand. I gave the word ' forward ' ; our little fellows were up like a shot, and advanced in beautiful order to the top of the hill. By way of bringing the enemy on, I sounded the *retreat*, having previously warned my men what I was going to do. It had the desired effect : on came the mutineers, and we met just as I got over the brow of the hill. I gave them one well-directed volley, and then ordered my guns to open. This sent them to the rightabout ; about fifty were killed, and a great number wounded. Had I been in greater force I think I should have succeeded in capturing the enemy's guns.

" We are under fire morning, noon, and night. We expect reinforcements from Umballah the day after to-morrow. We can hold our own, every attack having been at once repulsed ; two of my orderlies wounded to-day. ' Hindôo Rao's House ' very strong, but if they keep up the fire of their 32- and 24-pounders it cannot stand much longer. Heat very great; constant work and excitement keeps me in health. My little fellows are going to try their best to destroy the Bridge of Boats over the Jumna. Rather a difficult matter. They have already been down to it. They say it is well guarded, strong picquets on either side of the river, with double sentries in each boat. I fear they will not succeed; however, they will do their best."

June 16*th*.—" No attack to-day. The enemy busy erecting heavy batteries in 'Kissengunge.' I'm watching them closely. These batteries will enfilade the whole of my position."

June 17*th*.—" About 3 P.M. a 32-pounder round shot came smashing into the portico of the house which the officers occupy, killing Ensign Wheatley, 54th, who was doing duty with my regiment, a Havildar, and four of my men, besides two Carabineer orderlies, and a driver, and wounding Lieutenant Tulloch and three of my Goorkahs, one of whom (Ticca Ram) died that evening. (This little fellow was one of the best shots in the regiment. He had killed 22 tigers in the Dhoon. He was asleep, poor fellow, when he was wounded. Nine killed and four wounded by one round shot, and regimental colour cut in two.) About 3.30 I received orders from General Barnard to make a simultaneous attack with Major Tombs on the enemy's position outside the city, 'Kissengunge' and 'Trevelyan Gunge.' My column consisted of 4 companies 60th Royal Rifles, and my own regiment. The strength of the 4 companies of the 60th Rifles about 180. The Sirmoor Battalion 350 ; one company of the Sirmoors left at Hindôo Rao's House. I met Major Tombs' column at the cross road, when he took the right and I the left; my object was to get in the rear of the heavy batteries in 'Kissengunge,' which I effected by passing through two Serais, battering down three strong gates which were bricked up inside; and after crossing the new canal, and running down the bed of the old channel, we reached at length the gate in rear of the 'Kissengunge Serai,' which I found full of mutineers. The scaling ladders carried by the Sappers (20 in number, under Lieutenant Jones) were converted into a 'battering-ram,' and after some little trouble we succeeded in battering down the gate. The mutineers rushed on, sword in hand after firing their muskets; most of them appeared to be Sappers who were hard at work at the batteries: 31 were killed in one place, 19 in another, and at the very least 300 wounded. I destroyed their batteries and magazine, and after burning all the huts in the place, I withdrew, and reached Hindôo Rao's House about dusk. Total killed this day 7, and 8 wounded in Sirmoor's. The regimental colour was cut clean in two by the round shot which did so much havoc. The 60th Rifles in the attack on Kissengunge behaved admirably; the 4 companies were commanded by Captain J. R. Wilton, a fine gallant officer, who led his men in a manner which ensured confidence."

June 18th.—" I had General Barnard with me at nine o'clock last night. He came up to thank me for the affair of last evening, viz. the attack on 'Kissengunge.' It was a complete surprise, and very successful. An order of the General's thanking Major Tombs and self appeared in field force orders to-day. Another Lancer orderly of mine killed last night; 3 mounted orderlies killed out of *four* in two days, and two Goorkah orderlies wounded. Delhi will not be taken just at *present.*"

June 19*th.*—" I received a note this morning from Captain Curzon, Military Secretary, on the subject of the bridge of boats. If effectually destroyed, my men will receive six thousand rupees. The little fellows are most anxious to try what they can do; fifteen of them start to-night with combustibles. I am preparing cradles or rafts, on which I purpose placing Gurrahs filled with carcass composition. Two Gurrahs on each raft. These will be lighted, and taken off into the centre of the stream, and as the current is strong they will soon float down to the bridge of boats; but my only fear is, most of them will go through the gap left at night in the centre of the bridge. Four boats are taken out at night, which form picquet boats, placed about a hundred yards above and below the bridge. The jolly little fellows will start to-night. I hope to see them back all safe to-morrow, but I hardly think they will succeed. Notes constantly coming in from General Barnard, begging of me to keep a sharp look-out. The idea now is, so say our spies, to make a final struggle ere our reinforcements arrive. They talk of attacking our rear and front at the same time."

June 20*th*.—" No attack to-day on my position; the 'Moree,' 'Burn,' and 'Cashmere' Bastions are never silent. Each of these bastions mount from nine to twelve heavy guns; the 'Moree' is 1,200 yards from Hindôo Rao's House; the 'Burn,' 1,500; the 'Cashmere,' about the same: and the fire is principally directed against this house and neighbouring batteries."

June 21*st*.—" An attack made on our rear last evening. We captured one of the enemy's guns. Officers killed: Yule of the Lancers; Alexander, 3rd N.I., Colonel Becher, Quartermaster-General, Daly, Guides, and Williams, Rifles, wounded. On the Ridge we had nothing to say to this affair in the rear, being employed with another in our front. Several lives were lost."

" My men have returned from the bridge; five of them were missing all yesterday. They met a picquet of the mutineers whilst they were shoving the rafts across the river. They were fired upon; those who were able to dive went down like so many ducks, but the rest had to swim back. The divers, five of them, after some difficulty managed to get hold of the rafts again, and took them over to the left bank, where they lighted the port-fires, and set the rafts adrift; but, as I feared, most of them floated down the centre, and passed through the vacant space caused by the removal of the four boats. Two boats, however, took fire, and were with difficulty removed. However, the bridge was complete this morning. I get but little rest. My telescope is never hardly out of my hand during the day. The

'Bareilly Brigade' is expected to-day, when I conclude they will make one struggle more. We shall probably see them out on the 23rd, the anniversary of 'Plassey.'"

June 22nd.—"No attack to-day, but to-morrow we may expect the rascals out in force. 'Moree' very troublesome indeed, also 'Burn' Bastion. The enemy moving in my right rear. I'm watching them."

June 23rd.—"I was attacked early this morning. The enemy turned out in greater force than I have ever yet seen them. Prior to leaving the city they swore on the 'Gunga,' and 'Jumna jee,' that they would spike my heavy guns before sunset, and drive me out of 'Hindôo Rao's House.' They commenced by an attack on my right rear, having overnight occupied the buildings in the 'Subzee-mundee,' which we were not strong enough to hold. They had the advantage of the very best cover, the place being surrounded with jungle, and from the tops of the houses they completely commanded our right flank battery, which they were not long in taking advantage of. I soon discovered that the houses were full of infantry, and it became necessary to drive them out. I accordingly directed two companies of the 60th Rifles, three of my own regiment, and three companies of Guides to attack the place. They succeeded in driving the enemy out, but had not taken possession more than five minutes, when they were compelled to retire before a force some ten times their number. Immediately I saw my men retreating, I ordered the supports which were close to the buildings to advance. Again the enemy were driven back, and I had once again, after a hard struggle, possession of the buildings. I wrote off to Sir H. Barnard to say I required reinforcements; this was about 11 A.M., but none could he send me until about 2 P.M.; during this time I had the greatest difficulty in holding my own. The mutineers about 12 o'clock made a most desperate attack on the whole of my position. No men could have fought better. They charged the Rifles, the Guides, and my own men again and again, and at one time I thought I must have lost the day. The cannonade from the city, and the heavy guns which they had brought out raged fast and furious and completely enfiladed the whole of my position. Thousands were brought against my mere handful of men, but I knew the importance of my position, and was determined to do my utmost to hold it until reinforcements arrived. I drove the enemy out of their position in the 'Subzee-mundee' no less than six different times, and at length succeeded in establishing a small force in the place. We were fighting hard until sunset, when the mutineers gave it up as a bad job, and after withdrawing their heavy and light guns, which they had playing upon us the whole time, besides being under the fire of their heavy batteries (the Moree and Burn), they retired, leaving about 800 killed and wounded on the field. The loss in my own regiment in three weak companies, 36 killed and wounded. The Guides about the same. No report of the 60th Rifles as yet. Since the 8th I have lost 103 killed and wounded of my little fellows. At this rate I shall not have many left for *the* attack, which is not likely to take place just at present. I was struck by a spent ball on the spine to-day, but was not much hurt. The heat was excessive, and many of our men fell from the effects of the sun."

"I must here mention the conduct of my friend, 'Buddul Tappah' Jemadar, whom I promoted for his gallant conduct. I detached him with his company for the purpose of driving out the mutineers, who had taken possession of some buildings in the 'Subzee-mundee,' from which they completely enfiladed the whole of my position. He found a large body of the enemy in a high bricked wall enclosure, to which there was but one entrance, and the fire kept up upon it was so heavy that he found it impossible to advance through the gateway. He accordingly divided his company, placing half at the entrance, and with the remaining half he proceeded to the rear of the enclosure; here he substituted the back and shoulders of a Goorkah for a ladder, and in a wonderful short space of time he, with the men he took with him, were on the top of the wall firing down upon the enemy. The party left at the gate immediately rushed in, and thirty-five of the mutineers were killed on the spot, and a great number went away wounded. This was indeed a gallant and most daring achievement, especially as the company did not muster more than forty men. This man obtained the third class 'Order of Merit' for capturing a standard at 'Allewal.' He has now the second class order, and those who first scaled the wall in the novel style above described have the third class."

"Lieutenant Minto Elliot, of the Bengal Artillery, did admirable service with his two light guns, and he highly distinguished himself by a most conspicuous act of zeal and gallantry: aided by a sergeant and a gunner he worked a howitzer for several hours without relief of any sort or further assistance under a very heavy fire, which was almost incessant from the enemy's formidable bastions, as also from the musketry fire of the attacking force, his other light gun being at the time completely disabled. His coolness and daring shown on this occasion more than once attracted my notice; seven of the horses of his battery were killed, and seven wounded, and all his men were down with sunstroke and heat apoplexy.

"On hearing me express a wish on the 10th June to have an officer permanently attached to the two light guns at the picquet, Lieutenant Elliot volunteered to remain with me, which he accordingly did until the 23rd June, when he returned to camp with his disabled guns. His conspicuous gallantry on this occasion has been brought to notice, and I have recommended him for the 'Victoria Cross.'"

June 24th.—"A quiet day—glad of a little rest after our fight of yesterday. Coke's regiment not to be with us until the 29th. Had a letter from General Barnard this morning about the occupation of the 'Subzee-mundee.' The old gentleman does not apparently know where the place is. He says there is no object gained in extending our right, whereas the buildings are well in our right rear. If not held, certain it is that we must remove our right battery ; indeed, I much doubt whether I shall be able to hold Hindôo Rao's House. We must set to work with our defences ; a battery for my light guns, and breastworks are required. We cannot afford to lose men in the way we are doing. All well at the main picquet."

June 25th and 26th.—" No attack. The ' Moree ' and Burn Bastions always at work, and we lose a number of men here. Dangerous work moving from this house to the right battery. No cook boy can go from Hindôo Rao's House to the right flank battery without having half a dozen round shot fired at him ; they are wonderfully plucky fellows these cook boys of the 60th Rifles, and so are the ' Bheesties,' water carriers."

June 27th.—" We were attacked again this morning in greater force than ever. I occupied all the buildings in the ' Subzee-mundee,' consequently did not lose near so many men as on the 23rd. The enemy were somewhat astonished to find the place occupied. I lost to-day two killed and fourteen wounded ; detachment of 4th Seikhs, one killed and four wounded ; 180 of 2nd Fusiliers which I had in the ' Subzee-mundee,' fourteen killed and wounded. No report as yet of the 60th Rifles, or Guide Infantry. We were fighting for two hours in the rain, and very heavy it was. The rains have apparently set in, but Delhi is *not yet* taken, and not likely to be until we get more troops and heavy guns."

June 28*th*.—" Our reinforcements arrived this morning, such as they are; Coke's regiment not yet in. 'Moree' playing upon us."

June 29*th*.—" No attack to-day. 'Moree' at work as usual."

June 30*th*.—" The rascals were at us again this morning. The engagement did not last very long. I lost two of my little fellows killed and eleven wounded."

July 1*st*.—" The main picquet (I wish they would select some other by way of a change) was again attacked about noon to-day, and we were fighting till sunset, but with great good luck; I only lost two of my little fellows. I decided on taking up a new position some eighty paces in front of my old one. Stones and brushwood being at hand, I ran up a breastwork in the space of half an hour, and before the enemy could come round my flank, they found me prepared for them. I received most positive orders from Sir H. Barnard to act purely on the defensive, otherwise I should have made a rush for three of the enemy's guns, 9-pounders, which they brought out, and with which they annoyed us a good deal. The 60th Rifles is truly a fine regiment, so totally different to every other. My men are very fond of them, and they get on famously. We have lost about the same number of men up to this date; I have 28 killed, and 105 wounded—not to be wondered at, considering the rascals are always at us. John Coke's regiment will arrive to-morrow.

" The discipline in the 60th Royal Rifles was

perfect. I felt I could do anything with such men. My daily pencil reports, written either behind a rock or at the top of Hindôo Rao's House, recorded all that came under my observation at the time, and I was in hopes these reports, although written in pencil, would have been kept, and reference made to them when the final despatch of the siege was penned, but this, I regret to say, was not done. I more than once mentioned the names of officers of this noble regiment, who served under my command between the 8th June and 2nd August, during which time the crisis lasted.

"Finding that my pencil reports were taken no notice of, I sent in a supplementary despatch, in which I mentioned the names of Captain Hinxman, Captain Jones, Lieutenant Eaton, Lieutenant J. D. Dundas, Lieutenant H. G. Deedes, Lieutenant J. Hare, Lieutenant Ashburnham, and Lieutenant and Adjutant Kelly, all of the 60th Royal Rifles, who had done right good service on the Delhi Ridge : but I regret to say Lord Clyde replied, 'the time is altogether past for publishing any further despatches relative to these services, which, however meritorious, are now of old date.' I cannot, however, think that these services will be forgotten, at least I hope not. I likewise mentioned the names of several artillery officers who had served on the Ridge with me, but they appeared in my pencil reports, which were not in an 'official form,' though I certainly intended them as such. To have sat down daily to write long despatches on foolscap paper would have been an impossibility. I could watch the movements of the enemy and give my orders whilst writing pencil notes, but the 'official form' in ink was not possible. The particular services of the officers in the heavy batteries I left the field officer of artillery to mention, as I could not see all that was going on in the three different batteries, but all that came under my observation I mentioned."

July 2nd.—" The assault is to be made to-morrow morning an hour before daybreak. God grant it may be successful. The rascals have just knocked over our only 24-pounder : never mind, it will make no difference. Our guns are too far off to be of any use. We are replying with 18-pounders to their 24- and 32-pounders. It must be done with the bayonet after all. I get no rest at night, but nevertheless I am quite well. If I am attacked this evening the arrangements made for to-morrow will be upset ; it's almost impossible to say what force the enemy have, not less I should say than 20,000 mutineers. The followers of the prophet will of course fight, and are no doubt all armed. The 10th (my old regiment) gone at last : let them *all* go, say I."

July 3rd, 2 P.M.—" Just come in. The enemy made a night attack on my position. I acted on the defensive at first, but about daybreak I thought I might do something on the offensive. I drove them back, but they got up reinforcements and were soon seen coming up a second time to attack me. I turned the picquet out at 1 o'clock this morning, and have only just returned, so that we have been under arms for twelve hours and a half. Killing work. I have lost in all 138 of my little fellows, killed and wounded. I have written for my recruits from Deyrah, and furlough men."

July 3rd.—" On the afternoon of the 3rd July large bodies of insurgents moved into the large Gardens on my right rear and it became necessary to turn out the troops in camp. At night the enemy were still in force outside the city, and a movement was made upon 'Allipore,' one march in our rear. I had to watch the enemy closely the whole night, and my picquets were kept more alert than usual. About 2 A.M. a force marched under Major Coke to endeavour to intercept the mutineers. He had Money's troop of Horse Artillery, Scott's Horse Battery, a squadron of the Carabineers, a squadron of the 9th Lancers, a wing of 61st, and his own regiment, the 1st Punjaub Rifles; in all about 350 Cavalry, 800 Infantry, and 12 guns. About sunrise on the 4th July the enemy were seen coming back to Delhi, having plundered 'Allipore.' Coke at once moved to take them in flank, but had to proceed over most difficult ground for Artillery, the greater portion being swampy fields. He at length, however, came up with the enemy, who commenced moving off, whilst Coke's troops were forming up; he, however, succeeded in taking a quantity of small arm ammunition, and all the plunder taken by the mutineers at 'Allipore' was recaptured. Coke was unable to follow up the enemy owing to his having received strict orders not to cross the canal. On his return towards camp, whilst resting his men, he was attacked by some fresh troops which had moved out from Delhi to aid the retreat of the force returning from 'Allipore,' and it became necessary to send out from camp some Cavalry and Artillery to support Coke. The attack, however. had been repulsed before the reinforcement reached. Had Coke been permitted to use his own discretion he would have punished the enemy severely, but his hands were tied, General Barnard having directed him on no account to cross the canal."

"I was attacked on the 4th. It appears by the returns I lost three Goorkahs killed and six wounded."

July 9th.—" My time has been fully occupied in strengthening my position. The old House is rather shaky, it cannot stand much longer."

July 10th.—" We had another grand scrimmage yesterday ; the old story, an attack on my position. The enemy were about 8,000 strong, and fought desperately. The action commenced about half-past 7 o'clock in the morning, and was not over till 4 P.M. Hard rain the whole time. About 3 P.M. I wrote to Chamberlain, and begged to be allowed to act on the *offensive* ; that we had been the whole day under a very heavy fire of round shot, shell, and musketry, and that I did not think I should lose more men by doing a little business on the offensive ; anyhow I thought I should get rid of the scoundrels for the day. He agreed, and wrote saying he would himself try and turn their left flank, if I would turn their right, and drive them back into the city. I sent instructions for the latter movement to the officer commanding the Sammy House picquet. Away I went with five companies of my own regiment, two companies 60th Rifles under Sir E. Campbell, and 180 of the Guides under Shebbeare, in all about 750 men. We drove the enemy before us through the Jungle and down the Grand Trunk Road, where they were posted in thousands. About 400 yards from the city wall I halted, as I found I was getting my men under grape from the heavy guns in the ' Moree ' and ' Burn ' Bastions, as also from eight small guns which the mutineers had brought out, two of which were placed near the canal bridge. I was anxiously looking out for Chamberlain on my right. Presently he rode up himself, when I begged of him to send me guns. He rode off, and in about five minutes up came my old friend Major Scott with four 9-pounders. We were then able to return the fire of the enemy's light guns, which had annoyed us a good deal. After firing about half a dozen rounds from each gun I gave the order for another advance. The enemy evidently thought I was about to enter the city, for they not only withdrew their guns, but the whole of their infantry, and after entering by the ' Ajmere Gate ' they manned the walls, and commenced firing at me from the loopholes. At this time I was within 250 yards of the walls, but had got my men under good cover. I had fairly driven the enemy inside their walls, and as nothing more could be done with my handful of men we withdrew ; Scott's guns moving off so quietly that they could not have been

heard by the enemy. The Rifles, under Captain Sir
E. Campbell, who appears a first-rate officer, lost five
killed and ten wounded, Guides twenty killed and
wounded. A compay of the 2nd Fusiliers, which
came up with Scott's guns, five killed and wounded.
My own regiment, eight killed, one officer (Eckford),
and twenty-six wounded. Singheer Tappah, my
Sirdar Bahadoor, wounded through the neck, but is
doing well I'm happy to say. I got a crack over my
old head from something or other, but am not hurt.
The total loss in my regiment up to this date, 173.
High time I got some more men. We must have
killed a great number of the mutineers. Carts with
killed and wounded were seen going into the city
until dark. Our spies say their loss was very
great."

NOTES.—Many appeared to think that I ought to
have acted purely on the defensive until we were
ready to advance our batteries, but in my humble
opinion this would have been a very great mistake. The enemy would at once have thought
that we were afraid of them, and would have commenced a sneaking advance through the cover, the
like of which never was before seen; nearer and nearer
would they have brought their heavy and light guns
until they had at length completely surrounded us.
Their innumerable heavy guns and mortars were bad
enough as it was, but what would it have been had we
permitted them to approach still nearer ? I maintain
it was only by driving them back as I did on all occasions that we were able to hold the position we had

taken up before Delhi. Latterly their attacks were as feeble as they had at first been desperate; daily they became more and more disheartened; but would this have been the case had we entirely shut ourselves up within our defences? For my own part, I never would have acted for one moment on the defensive, situated as we were. When a sortie was made I would at once have met it, but at the same time taking care, as I always did, not to get my men under grape range of the heavy bastions; but it will be seen I was overruled latterly, and had often to act on the defensive, which always had a bad effect upon the Sikhs and Goorkahs. One day one of my little fellows, who had just lost his brother, said, " Sahib, here we are getting knocked over in cold blood; do let us jump over this breastwork and go at the enemy. They think we are afraid of them." " Have patience," was my reply, "and get under cover; I'll let you go presently;" upon which he gave a broad grin, and looked quite happy.

July 11*th*.—" The only birthday present I can send you from this is a Punjab medal, which was taken from the breast of one Jankee Singh, Sepoy of the 18th N.I. who fought on the 9th, and who was killed by one of my little fellows at the commencement of the action, with many more of that distinguished Corps, which formed part of the ' Bareilly Brigade,' the whole of which turned out on that day, and fought most desperately."

" The enemy came out again yesterday, but seeing I was prepared for them they retired. Heat fearful, and many knocked down by the sun."

July 12*th.*—" All quiet except the old 'Moree Bastion,' which annoys us a good deal. Received a note from Chamberlain, saying that the enemy intend to pay me another visit to-day. All ready for them, but I don't think they intend an attack to-day ; I can generally tell when they are coming out by the strength of their picquets in ' Kishengunge ' and ' Pahareepore.' My idea is, they won't attack again until they get another Brigade. Perhaps the 10*th N.I.* may have a try to take Hindôo Rao's with their four colours. I shall know them immediately. Heavy rain ; enemy's heavy batteries very troublesome."

July 13*th.*—" Hodson writes me—' Colonel Becher desires me to tell you that the " Pandies " have sworn to take your batteries and position this time positively : what a bore for you ! They are all armed and accoutred, and ready to turn out, but the time does not seem to be fixed. As your next appearance will be in Delhi I suppose, I have only to say good-bye.' They have tried to take my batteries and position nineteen different times. They may succeed the twentieth, but I have my doubts. All ready for the rascals : our spies say the enemy lost 1,500 killed and wounded on the 9th ; that they are busy this morning collecting firewood. No move in their camp which is pitched near the Ajmere Gate ; they have not room, apparently, for all the scoundrels inside the city."

July 14*th.*—" Fighting all day. The engineers were hard at work last night in strengthening the walls of the old House, which is riddled through and through with shot and shell. The 32-pound shot

D

from the 'Burn' Bastion go clean through the walls."

July 15*th*.—" I was attacked again yesterday, the twentieth time; they had sworn all sorts of things, they would this time take my batteries and post, and succeed they must. The attack commenced at 8 o'clock in the morning, and we were fighting hard until 6 P.M. At 4 o'clock Chamberlain wrote me to drive the enemy back, and to act in concert with him; that he would take them in flank if I would attack them in front. We drove them into the city, but they succeeded in getting us under the fire of grape from the ' Moree' and ' Burn' Bastions. We suffered severely—in fact, lost as many, if not more, than the enemy. Chamberlain severely wounded. The enemy were in great force between the 'Sammy House' and 'Pahareepore,' where they had light guns. I was requested by Chamberlain to cover the retreat. Our H.A. guns moved off at a gallop, making such a noise on the Pucka Road that the enemy at once discovered, though they could not see us, that we were retreating; they consequently came out again in force, and we had to drive them back a second time, not however without great loss to ourselves. I cannot say what we lost in all. I had three officers wounded, Ross, Chester, and Tulloch, the latter severely, and 34 of my fine little fellows killed and wounded. I was struck by a spent ball on the shin bone, somewhat painful; a 24-pounder shot shaved my old head, but thank God it's still on my shoulders. I must have more men at this picquet, otherwise I cannot hold the position; these constant attacks have thinned my ranks considerably. My total loss killed and wounded, since the 8th June, 216, nearly half the regiment."

July 16*th*.—" Every prospect of being quiet to-day. Beecher's spies say not! We are working away at the 'Sammy House;' for the future I shall call it 'Fort Sammy.' There never was such ground, nothing but rock and jungle, which of course affords the enemy good cover. Baird Smith writes me that he will do his best for me in the way of clearing jungle and throwing up breastworks. I have got a light gun battery close to this house, which Baird Smith got run up for me in a couple of hours on the morning of the 14th; the work was placed in Taylor's hands, and he certainly did not disappoint me or his chief. I must agitate for more troops at this post; the whole brunt of every attack falls on my position, and as Baird Smith says, 'No better use of the troops could be made than to strengthen your hands.'"

July 17*th*.—" The 'Moree' and 'Burn' Bastions continue to send me their iron messengers, and the old house shakes again."

July 19*th*.—" The 'Pandies,' as they are called, made their *twenty-first* attack on my position yesterday. They swore all kinds of things on the holy waters of the 'Gunga,' that they would have my post, and that before sunset the people in the city would see me—the Prince of Devils, as they call me in the Green Turban—hung in the 'Chandnee Chowk.' ' If the infantry could not manage to take Hindôo

Rao's House, the cavalry would.' They turned out of the city at half-past seven o'clock in the morning, and kept us at it until dark. Not a thing had we to eat, and we all came home dead beat. I never was so completely done up before. The sun about 2 o'clock was something fearful. We were acting on the defensive until 4 o'clock, when I received an order from Wilson (who is made a Brigadier General, and has taken command) to advance. He directed me to drive the enemy from my front and left. This was done pretty sharply by the troops now under me—viz. 180 of the 8th and 61st Queen's, 120 of 60th Rifles, 318 of Coke's Regt., and 200 of my little fellows, which is all I now have, alas ! We drove the enemy within their strong walls, but they again came up to their cover, which is not to be described. I lost fifteen killed and wounded of my little fellows. Thank goodness, I expect 91 from Deyrah : I wish I had a thousand coming. General Reed has left for Simla. His farewell order was issued yesterday. I enclose a copy of one para. The enemy have got reinforcements, and talk of coming out again to attack my position : they hope to wear me out."

July 24*th*.—" The enemy were pleased to attack us again yesterday, but they were not very desperate, and, beyond bringing out four light guns to play upon my position, and a lot of men with rifles to snipe at us from a distance behind stone walls and thick jungle, they did not further molest me. Nevertheless they had me out at 8 o'clock in the morning, and I did not return to the old house until 5 P.M. So long as they are outside the city in force I can never move; were I to do so, they would instantly make a rush at my batteries. Some two or three thousand turned out of the Cashmere Gate at the same time and attacked the Mosque picquet, as also Metcalfe's picquet. These were ordered to advance, and drive the enemy back, which was done pretty sharply; but our loss in officers was very great: poor Law killed, Colonel Seaton wounded, Colonel Drought wounded, Captain Money and three other officers slightly wounded. Poor Law was with Coke's Regiment; he died, as every soldier would wish to die, in front of his men, sword in hand, making a rush at the enemy. He had been with me on the Ridge for about a week, and such confidence had I in him that I gave him command of the 'Sammy House' picquet. A better soldier never lived, and I feel his loss greatly. I wish we had a few more like him. I have three light mortars for the 'Crow's Nest,' which did good service yesterday. I am cutting away at jungle as fast as I can, and daily making my position stronger. Heavy rain to-day; the enemy just now quiet, but hard at work repairing batteries. We shall not take Delhi before we get reinforcements in infantry and guns."

July 28*th.*—" As soon as the mutineers have had their dinner they are coming out in great force, and are determined *this time* to take my batteries and position! All quiet as yet, and no move in the Ajmere Gate direction. Our wounded start this evening for Deyrah. The enemy got large reinforcements on Sunday last—the Neemuch, Mhow, Agra, and a portion of Gwalior mutineers, some ten thousand in all, with eight or ten guns. The King ordered them to march straight on, and to take up a position in our rear at Allypore or Raee; however, instead of obeying the orders of His Majesty, they pitched their camp close to the old city of Delhi; they, however, struck it yesterday morning, and where they are gone to I cannot make out—not in our rear, certainly, at least not within six miles, for that distance I can see with a telescope from my 'look-out.'* Our spies still think the enemy are coming out: 15,000 of them, with 100 guns; and that after taking my position, they take the camp; but the great day of all is to be the 1st proximo, the Eed! Come when they will, I am all ready for them; and, please God, they will not, after all, carry me off a prisoner to the Imperial City, which they say they are particularly anxious to do. My recruits have arrived all safe."

July 29*th.*—" I was not attacked after all yesterday. All quiet this morning. I fancy they will leave me alone until the 'Eed.' We used to send a guard to prevent disturbances during this festival; I wonder if they would like us to send one this time. My poor wounded men left this in carts last evening, the Sirdar Bahadoor at their head. I fear he will not live, he has a bad wound through the neck. Cholera in the city, our spies say, and fever too. The more the better, eh? Please God, we shall thus get rid

---

* I have four Goorkahs at the top of the Hindôo Rao's House always on the look out. Nicholson asked me if they lived there, and if they ever get anything to eat.

of a thousand or two of the scoundrels. It is not bad in our camp. I have had no cases at my picquets. Poor Ross was a great loss to me; he would have made a first-rate adjutant. The very day he died, my order appointing him to officiate came back confirmed. His wound had nothing to say to his death. He died of cholera. Eckford I hope to see back from the general hospital in a day or two. Tulloch has gone to Mussoorie, his wound is a very severe one."

August 1st.—" Here I am writing by candlelight at 8 A.M. It reminds me of poor Brother John's cabin on board the *Colossus*. It has been raining very heavily since 12 o'clock yesterday, and it is so dark we cannot see without a candle. The enemy came out in great force yesterday, with the intention of making a grand attack on front, rear, right, and left! They came out of the Ajmere Gate like so many bees. 'Sorbea,' my head look-out man, came to tell me that the whole of Delhi had turned out. I went up to take a look round, and found it necessary to sound the 'alarm' at once. About ten thousand, with six H.A. guns, four 9-pounders, materials for making bridges, &c., were seen coming up in my direction. Away I went with my troops to take up my old position on the right and left of the right flank battery. Presently, I saw another large force coming round my right, and making direct for the Rhotuck Road. This force was evidently intended to make the rear attack; but they had a task before them which they did not much relish, viz. constructing a bridge over the canal. They were busy at it until noon, when down came the heaviest rain I ever saw. While this force was at work, trying what they could do in our rear, some three thousand infantry, with four light guns, attacked me in front and right flank, but they would not come close up, and in fact had no intention of making an actual attack until they could make a combined one on *all sides*. They had the advantage over us, the scoundrels, in point of keeping themselves and their ammunition *dry*, as they were able to get into the Kissengunge buildings, whereas we were exposed to the heaviest rain until 5 P.M., when the combined attack was given up as a bad job, and they retreated with their guns, and we, poor drowned rats, to our quarters in Hindôo Rao's House. About 1 o'clock heavy mortars were taken out to the force in our rear. Elephants, camels, covered carts, &c., laden with tents, ammunition, baggage, &c., so that they were determined to make themselves comfortable. A 24-pounder round shot *just* came through one of the upper rooms and killed one of my poor little fellows. The poor fellow cut completely in two. The poor old house is now somewhat shaky. I must have more sandbags placed to-night to strengthen the walls. The rascals are now coming out, so I must put down my pencil. Just come down from my lookout. About one thousand of the enemy firing from the buildings in ' Kissengunge.' I won't turn out for them ; my picquets are quite strong enough. I had another orderly killed yesterday. He was standing by my side in the right flank battery, and I was, at the time, holding out my telescope to him when a 24-pounder round shot took his head clean off, and then passed through the body of a 'Peepawalla,' who was carrying my serai of tea, which was kept pretty warm by the heat of the sun! I should have preferred it cold I must say. Perfectly wonderful how I escape. Round shot, shell, and musket balls come phit, phit, phee, phish, past my old head, but still here it is all safe on my shoulders."

August 3rd.—" Here I am, all safe after the grand 'Eed attack' which was entirely on my position. The engagement commenced at sunset on the 1st, lasted the whole night and until 4 P.M. yesterday. The mutineers tried very hard to get in our rear as I mentioned in my letter of the 1st. They managed to erect a bridge across the canal at Bussie, but it was carried away by the flood. Their guns were for some time left on one side, and Infantry and Cavalry on the other. This report was sent me by the General about 4 P.M. on the 1st, about half an hour after I saw the whole force returning, guns, mortars, &c. The mutineers were joined by about three or four thousand from the city, and the whole force, in all about 20,000, came straight at my position. I was prepared for them. The General sent up my supports sharp as he always does, and we commenced work. The 'Sammy House' was first attacked by about 5,000. At this time I had only 150 of Coke's men in it under Travers, and fifty of the Guides. I at once sent them reinforcements from the Rifles and 61st Queen's. At dusk the enemy brought up their guns, supported by a very large force, and then commenced the sharpest fire I have ever heard on the whole of my position. They were very desperate indeed. Before 12 o'clock we drove them back half-a-dozen times; the firing then ceased for about a quarter of an hour, and I began to think I had got rid of my friends; but shortly after the moon rose, which they apparently had been waiting for, up came fresh troops from the city bugling and shouting on all sides. I passed the word from right to left to allow the enemy to come close up and to keep a dead silence in the ranks. On came the enemy with their light guns up the Grand Trunk Road, as also up the Kissengunge Road. My three light guns which were in battery across the road were all loaded with grape, and when the enemy were close up they opened, and round after round with volleys of musketry from the 'Sammy House' had the effect of driving them back again. Still there they were within four hundred yards of me making preparations for another attack, whilst their light guns kept up one continued blaze, as also their heavy guns from the 'Moree' and 'Burn' Bastions. This sort of thing went on the whole night, but I managed to hold my own with four companies 60th Rifles 180 strong, 180 of the 8th and 61st Queen's, 200 Sirmoor Battalion, 300 Guides, and 150 of Coke's men, in all 910, against, at the very least, 20,000. My troops behaved admirably, all were steady and well in hand, and I never for one moment had any doubts about the result. At daybreak, more troops were seen in the Kissengunge buildings, and on they came again at the 'Sammy House.' I accordingly sent Sir E. Campbell with a company of the 60th Rifles to reinforce the troops at that post. At 8 A.M. they gave us time to get a little breakfast, but before 9 o'clock on they came again, and it was not before 5 P.M. last evening that I had the satisfaction of seeing them in full retreat, guns and all. Thus ended the great Eed attack, being number twenty-four on my position. Poor Travers, Coke's second in command, was killed in the Sammy House. I have no return as yet of killed and wounded, and I dread looking at the reports. The enemy's loss must have been very severe. The escapes I have had are perfectly wonderful. People look at me after every engagement and say: 'What, are you still untouched?' Thank God for thus sparing me. I hope to keep my old head on my shoulders for some time yet; anyhow until I have seen the imperial city fall. These persevering villains seem determined to wear us out; our spies say they are coming out again; all ready for them."

> Notes.—On my way back to Hindôo Rao's House I saw a boy squatting behind a rock with a rifle in his hand. I approached him, on which he got up and saluted me, and said, "I am a Line boy, and came here with the recruits. I have disobeyed orders, Sahib, but I could not help it. My father was on duty in the Sammy House, and I went down there to assist him in getting out his cartridges. He was killed, and I then went to one of the 60th Rifles to help him in loading quickly.

Notes—*cont.* He was shortly afterwards wounded. He gave me his rifle, and told me to get a 'Doolie' and send him to the hospital. I did so, and then went at it myself. After firing a few shots a bullet struck me which has made *four holes* in my legs, but I am not much hurt." He looked *quite* pleased, and I fancy saw by the expression of my face that I was not very angry at his having disobeyed orders in leaving the Dhoon. I enlisted him then and there, and sent him to the hospital. The bullet had passed through the fleshy part of both his thighs without touching bone, and I don't think he was more than ten days in hospital. Indeed, the surgeon had difficulty in keeping him there, such was the boy's pluck. He was one of the Fighting class of Goorkah, and was at the time not more than twelve or thirteen years of age. The *esprit de corps* shown by these Line boys throughout the siege was wonderful. Out of twenty-five men who obtained the Order of Merit for Delhi, twelve were Line boys, and out of seven who received the order for "Allewal" and "Sobraon," five were Line boys. Only those of Goorkah parentage were enlisted, and I never found they deteriorated in the least, or were in any way inferior to the pure Goorkah from Nepaul. They are naturally loyal to the State as *their regiment is their home.*

" It was a glorious victory, and I cannot speak too highly of the conduct of the troops under my command. Our spies say the enemy is very much disheartened, they made sure of success. They are after mischief, I see, in 'Kissengunge.' I dare say they think

I can't see them at work. More batteries to enfilade my position. I must have my earthworks at the 'Sammy House' and 'Crow's Nest' strengthened, they are only musket proof; my Goorkahs have erected all the defences between the 'Crow's Nest' and 'Subzee-mundee.' I have working parties out every night."

August 4th.—" Very busy to-day. Only time to say that I'm all right, never felt better in my life. I am sending in a report of my last fight."

August 5th.—" The mutineers had an inspection parade this morning outside the Ajmere Gate. We heard their bands playing some lively airs, such as 'Cheer, boys, cheer,' 'The girls we left behind us,' 'The British Grenadiers,' &c. This was more than I could stand, and I tried to send some shells amongst them, but they all fell short. News from the city states they are dreadfully disheartened at the result of their grand 'Eed attack ;' they still talk of a move to our rear. They will find Nicholson in their way."

" This morning five bales of flannel shirts, blouses, shoes, &c., arrived from Mussoorie for my Goorkahs ; the good ladies at that place, on hearing that the little fellows were in rags, held a meeting, when it was decided that they should themselves provide for our wants, and a subscription should be got up amongst the ladies of Landour and Mussoorie, and that they should daily meet for the purpose of working, cutting out shirts, blouses, &c., with their own hands. This was indeed very gratifying, and truly grateful

were the little fellows to the ladies for their great
kindness and consideration. We at once turned out
in our new suits of coloured shirts and blouses, and
it was amusing to witness the look of wonderment
the Pandies gave us. They evidently were taken by
surprise, and thought I had an increase to my force on
the Ridge. Even our old friends the Rifles did not
know us again, so smart had we turned out in our new
garb. The feeling which existed between the men of
the 60th Rifles and my own men was admirable ; they
called one another ' brothers,' shared their grog with
each other, and smoked their pipes together. Often
were the Rifles seen carrying a wounded Goorkah
off the field, and *vice versâ*. They had marched
together from the banks of the Hindun, and had
fought side by side for so long that they became
quite attached to one another. My men used to
speak of them as ' our Rifles,' and the men of the
60th, when mentioning the Goorkhas, ' them Gurkees
of ours.' Notwithstanding this good feeling there
was a good deal of rivalry. My men would never
allow that they were in any way inferior to the
Rifles. The emulation consequently was great, and
I had always the feeling that I could do almost anything with such men. One was always striving to
get ahead of the other, of which I had pretty good
proof on the 17th of June, when I drove the enemy
out of the strong loopholed Serai of ' Kissengunge.' I
may here mention what an officer of H.M.'s 10th
Regt. said of my men after the battle of ' Sobraon.'
He said he had watched the Goorkahs throughout

the engagement, and more especially when we came to close quarters with the Seikhs in their entrenchments, and he felt pretty confident that a regiment of Europeans, and a well-disciplined corps of Goorkahs would do more together in the field than any two corps of Europeans. I remarked that the Goorkah had not quite the physical strength of the European, to which he replied, 'No ; but they have as much pluck ; and the *esprit de corps* in your regiment, I see, is very great.' Here he was right ; and this is what I have ever tried to keep up. Indeed, without it I consider a regiment is good for nothing. When a corps has made a name for itself in the field, the men of course know it at the time ; but I say, don't let them forget it. Let every recruit who is enlisted understand that he has joined a good fighting regiment, and that if he does not possess sufficient pluck to keep up the name of the regiment he had better walk off somewhere else. Impress this on every man when he enlists, and you at once instil that *esprit de corps* which is so much needed in our army. Let every man know what is expected of him in the field ; that he must ever be ready to shed his last drop of blood for his Queen and his country ; and moreover, that he must never disgrace the *name* of his regiment. The difference in corps of our army is very remarkable ; in some regiments the discipline is all that could be desired, and the *esprit de corps* great ; in others you see little or none. And why is this ? The men are the same. You may see finer men in one regiment than you do in another ; but you ought not to see less discipline, or *esprit de corps*; if you do the officers are at fault. The discipline in some regiments is remarkably good in cantonments; but the misfortune is they don't take it with them into the field. Some of the detachments I have had with me on the Ridge have positively shown no discipline at all whilst under fire; but I have always blamed the officers, not the men."

Notes.—The best disciplined regiments we had at Delhi were the 9th Lancers and 60th Royal Rifles. A little incident occurred one day on the Ridge, which showed what the Lancers were in this respect. I had always two Cavalry orderlies at Hindôo Rao's House, and one morning I went out to meet the enemy coming over the Ridge and told the two Lancer orderlies to follow me. When I got to the Crow's Nest Picquet, I directed them to dismount and get behind a rock with their horses where there was good cover, and to remain there until I sent for them. After I had driven the enemy back I returned to Hindôo Rao's House, and forgot all about the Lancer orderlies. The next morning I had occasion to write to the General and directed the letter to be given to one of the orderlies to be taken to the camp. The Goorkah looked at me and said: "They are not here, Sahib, they are where you left them yesterday, near the Crow's Nest." I sent for them at once, and gave them great praise for having so strictly obeyed my orders, and reported the incident to the General. It afterwards turned out that they had had no dinner the day before and no breakfast that morning.

Notes—*cont.* This the Goorkah informed me. The men themselves did not say a word about it! Would that I could have seen the same discipline in every regiment.

August 9th.—" I thought these rascals had had enough of it after the thrashing I gave them on the 1st and 2nd ; but it appears not. They attacked me again on the morning of the 6th, and we have been under arms ever since ; they came out in great force, and took up a position in 'Kissengunge,' the same 'Serai' I turned them out of on the 17th June, which is close to my right flank. They erected a battery for heavy guns during the night of the 6th, and at daybreak on the 7th they commenced pounding me with two 24-pounders ; this went on the whole of the 7th, yesterday, and again to-day. One battery was not sufficient, so they commenced another, a sunken battery, about an hour ago, and they will have two more heavy guns in position by daybreak to-morrow. These two batteries are within 600 yards of 'Hindôo Rao's House,' and enfilade the whole of my position. The breastworks which I had repaired the other day have been knocked to pieces. As far as I can make out they have now four heavy guns in position, and will have more to-morrow. We must silence these guns, otherwise I cannot hold the Ridge. We are pounding away at 'Kissengunge,' but cannot silence their guns."

" Whilst writing General Wilson a hurried line in pencil, General Nicholson came up with Major Norman. I had never seen him before in my life, and I thought

I had never seen a man I disliked so much at first sight. His haughty manner and peculiar sneer I could not stand. He asked several questions relative to the enemy's position, and then passed on. Baird Smith was with me at the time, having come up to see if he could do anything for me in the way of strengthening my breastworks. I complained of Nicholson's overbearing manner. He replied, ' Yes, but that wears off. I'm sure you'll like him when you have seen more of him.' So I found it, and we became the best of friends. He was often with me, and I liked him exceedingly. He used often to come up in the dead of night if there was more firing than usual, and asked me if I required more men ; that if I did, to send to him, and not trouble the General. One night he sat with me on the top of Hindôo Rao's House, whilst a pretty sharp fire was going on. The 'Sammy House' picquet had been attacked, and the 'Moree,' as usual, took it up, and fired showers of grape from the left face of the bastion. It was nothing unusual. The same thing had gone on night after night from the first, and I suggested that he had better go back to camp, and go to bed. After some little time, he said : ' Reid, you have got rather too many Seikhs on the Ridge ; take my advice, and get the General to relieve some of them. They are all very well in their way, and fight remarkably well, but don't place too much confidence in them. No man knows them better than I do.' I had previously told him of the parley that had gone on at the 'Sammy House' between our Seikhs and the Seikhs who were with the enemy, of whom there were about two thousand. I told him it had made me feel very uneasy at times, and that at that very moment I had 600 Seikhs on the Ridge out of 1,060 men, which I then had under my command. He said again, 'Get some of them relieved. Good-night. If you want aid, send one of your orderlies to me.' After this he used often to come up, calling out from the bottom of the ladder, which led to my 'look-out'—'Have I permission to pass this sentry of yours? He always stops me.' The last time I saw the fine fellow was on the morning of the 13th September, when he came up to make arrangements with me regarding the assault next morning, where we were to meet, &c., that he would open the 'Cabool Gate' for me from the inside, after I had taken 'Kissengunge,' 'Trevelyangunge,' and 'Peharcepore,' &c. But, alas! I never saw his noble face again. The Bengal Army had need be proud of such a man as John Nicholson."

August 11th.—" I returned from the breastwork at the Crow's Nest yesterday at 2 P.M. They are tolerably quiet to-day, so I take the opportunity of retiring to my den in this house in order to have a little rest, which I find I am in need of, having been out since the 6th. The villains have found out the way to worry us. We have four heavy guns and six heavy mortars playing on the Kissengunge batteries, which annoy us very much, as they are within 600 yards and enfilade the whole of my position; but we are unable to silence them. They have directed their fire on the 'Sammy House,' and this house which they have got the range of. One of my poor little fellows lost his head by a round shot about five minutes ago. The poor old house is getting knocked to pieces. Hold it I must, so we must strengthen the walls with sandbags. My total loss in the regiment up to this date, 249 killed and wounded. Poor little fellows!"

August 12th.—" This morning the General sent out a small force to capture some guns which were annoying the Metcalfe picquet. It was admirably done, and a complete surprise; four guns were taken and a good number of the enemy killed. Showers commanded, who was wounded, as also my dear friend John Coke; but neither seriously. Sheriff, of the 2nd Europeans, killed. Kissengunge batteries annoying me a good deal; they completely enfilade my position."

> **Notes.**—The enemy having established themselves in "Ludlow Castle" and planted a battery which contrived greatly to harass our picquet in the Metcalfe House, it was deemed desirable to dislodge him. I had watched the construction of the battery from the top of Hindòo Rao's House, and before it opened fire I pointed out to General Wilson the earthworks which had been erected, as also the site of the battery. He told me he had decided on turning the enemy out of "Ludlow Castle," and that a column under Brigadier Showers would start early on the morning of the 12th with that object in view. He directed me to aid Showers in his attack in

Notes—*cont.* the event of the enemy being reinforced from the city, but not otherwise, as my troops on the Ridge would be greatly exposed, and would come under the fire of " Moree " and " Cashmere " Bastions, as also the fire of the loopholed curtain walls. Brigadier Showers accordingly, before the dawn of day, started with his column, 75th Foot, 1st Bengal Fusiliers, Coke's Punjab Rifles, and a battery of light field guns. Coke was directed to take his regiment through the Metcalfe Compound, and attack the enemy's works to the left of the main road, whilst Showers, with the other portion of the column, moved down the Grand Trunk Road on " Ludlow Castle." Coke's object was to get as near " Ludlow Castle " as possible without being seen, so he took advantage of the shelter afforded by a high wall which ran parallel to the main road; and in due course, after meeting with some opposition, he got opposite Ludlow Castle gate. Here he found the enemy on the alert—they had lined the wall round the Compound, and they instantly opened fire on his men. In order to drive the enemy from the shelter afforded them, and get into the Ludlow Castle enclosure, he had to get out of the Metcalfe Park, which there was some difficulty about, owing to the height of the wall. At length he discovered a hole in it which had been made by our round shot from the Ridge batteries. Through this Coke managed to creep, followed by a number of his men, and he made a rush for the gate, from which he was able to enfilade the enemy lining the walls of " Ludlow Castle." Here he fell with a gunshot wound

Notes—*cont.* through his thigh, but he was up again immediately, and presently saw one of the enemy's Horse Artillery guns standing on the road in front of him. The gunners and drivers had been shot down, but there stood the gun with the four horses, and their heads turned towards the Cashmere Gate. Coke at once saw that we should lose the gun unless their heads were turned *towards Camp*, so he walked up to the leaders as best he could and quietly turned the gun round on the road, and started the horses off, full gallop, without riders, and in they went straight into our camp. Showers meanwhile on the right of the Grand Trunk Road completely took the enemy by surprise, and numbers were shot down before they could man their guns. Some drew their swords, and, with their backs against the walls of Ludlow Castle, sold their lives dearly. Sherriff, 2nd Europeans, killed ; Showers and Coke severely wounded. We thus lost the services for the remainder of the siege of two most valuable officers.

Demi Official.
Main Picquet, Hindôo Rao's House,
August 12*th*, 1857.

MY DEAR GENERAL,—My report of the attack on my position on the night of the 1st and morning of the 2nd inst. was a hurried affair ; but I am, indeed, glad you have given me an opportunity of bringing to notice the names of officers and men who have served under me since the 8th June last. I cannot speak too highly of the conduct of the detachments of the 60th Royal Rifles, who have, on all occasions, behaved admirably, and ever maintained the reputation of their distinguished corps. I would wish to bring to your notice the names of two officers of this regiment, viz. Captain Sir E. Campbell and Captain J. R. Wilton, who have, at different times, commanded the parties on duty at this post, and from whom I have always received the greatest assistance. Both are most excellent officers, and I beg to recommend them to notice.

My acknowledgments are due to Lieutenant R. H. Shebbeare, now commanding the distinguished corps of Guides, who has been three times slightly wounded while on duty with me. Also to Lieutenant Hawes, Adjutant, likewise wounded, and other officers doing duty with the corps.

Detachments of the 1st Punjaub Infantry and 4th Seikhs have, since their arrival in camp, been constantly on duty at this post, and have always behaved, on all occasions of attack, with gallantry.

To Lieutenant Fisher, the second in command of my own regiment, and the officers doing duty, my warmest thanks are due. The conduct of the men you have already been pleased to make honourable mention of. It only remains for me to say that they have done their duty most cheerfully.

My thanks are also due to the officers and men of H.M.'s 8th and 61st Regiments, who have at

different times taken the duties at the "Subzeemundee picquet," which is under my command.
Yours sincerely,
CHARLES REID, *Major*,
Commanding " Advanced Picquets."
To *Brigadier General Wilson,*
Commanding Delhi Field Force.

August 13*th.*—" Kissengunge batteries still pounding me. They have knocked my breastworks to pieces, and Fort Sammy is in a bad way. We are not in sufficient force, otherwise we ought to take and occupy 'Kissengunge.' It is a very strong place, but there would be no object in taking it unless we are prepared to hold it, which we are not. They would only bring out more guns immediately we retired."

August 14*th.*—" Kissengunge very troublesome. The enemy give me no rest ; they had me up twice last night ; they came up within twenty paces of this house. It was so dark the picquets could not see them. I only hope they felt our grape ! "

August 15*th.*—" The enemy have got in our rear again. Nicholson went out with a force last evening and will attack them this evening I fancy. The villain who has set himself up at 'Boolundshur' is my friend 'Wully dad Khan,' who has a small fort at 'Malagur.' I had the pleasure of pitching two of his guns down a well at 'Boolundshur.' I was very nearly paying him a visit whilst I was at Boolundshur, but Sapte told me he was not worth it. I accordingly sent my compliments to him, and requested him to send his guns to me. Next morning they arrived, but having no powder to burst them, I threw them down a well."

August 16th.—" The heavy guns in Kissengunge annoy me a good deal. We cannot silence them. Funny state of things, 24- and 18-pounder shot are sent at our heads with our *own* guns, and we hurl them back again at the enemy! The *same* shot go backwards and forwards until they are quite worn out. 'Look at this, sir,' said a gunner to me the other day, holding up a 24-pounder shot. 'She's pretty nearly done for, she's oval instead of round.' 'Never mind, my man; send it at the villains once more.' Bang went the gun, and the shot into the Kissengunge batteries; and so goes on this game of pounding with round shot and shell, hammer and tongs. We are very well and very happy at the 'Main Picquet.' They have made the 'Moree' Bastion stronger than ever. Counter guards, inner parapets, embrasures for more guns &c.; never mind, when once we commence with 40 heavy guns we shall make short work of it."

August 17th.—" By way of strengthening 'Kissengunge,' the enemy have thrown a breastwork across the road, near the canal bridge, and another across the old channel of the canal. Yesterday they were pretty quiet, and I am rejoiced to say we did not lose a man. Heavy rain all night and again this morning; wretched work for men on picquet duty. I have now 1,060 men on duty at my picquets, and am ready for the *whole* of Delhi. They pound me with their heavy and light guns, but have of late given up attacking me."

A little incident worthy of note occurred on the morning of this day. About a quarter of an hour before our usual breakfast time, Dr. Morris's table attendant came into the portico with a very long face, followed by my own "khit" (table attendant) trembling from head to foot ; something had evidently happened, and at length out it came. A 24-pounder round shot had passed through the kitchen immediately over the stove on which was placed our breakfast stew. It was not knocked over, our "khits" informed us, but it was full of plaster and mortar, and sundry pieces of brick. This was a trifle compared with the intelligence that followed; it appeared that before the shot made its exit through the opposite wall of the kitchen it must needs travel through a box in which was placed, amongst other articles of use, all the delicacies of the season, and which had just been sent to us by Messrs. Peak, Allan and Co., from Umballah. Out came a mug in all manner of shapes, then a piece of salmon tin, and so on. All, of course, were in fits of laughter, but the poor "khits," who had had a narrow escape, did not appear to see the fun at all. Several shots had before struck the cook room, but this iron messenger was the only one that had done any real mischief. It was sent to us by friends in "Kissengunge," and apparently from the sunken battery, which always gave great annoyance. The "khits," after being laughed into good humour, went back to the "stew," which, after all, was not so bad, though pronounced somewhat gritty.

Little incidents of this nature occurred frequently. On one occasion my "Bunneahs" (grain sellers) had procured a large quantity of flour from the camp, and this they had heaped up in front of one of the outhouses, when all of a sudden there was a thud, then an explosion, and immediately after up went a white cloud of flour! A ten-inch shell had fallen right into the centre of the heap, and had there burst. On another occasion a shell from "Kissengunge" went through our tents, which were all packed and piled up in a heap near the house. It was amusing to see them when they were afterwards pitched; there was certainly no want of ventilation! At first the "Pandies" could not get their shells to burst, consequently we did not care much about them; but they soon found out that the fuses were not properly secured, and this was speedily rectified. The old house was a good mark for them, but providentially no shell found its way into the "Expense Magazine," which was under the right wing of the house, and where we had a very large quantity of powder, at one time as much as 10,000 lbs., shells, rockets, &c.

August 18*th*.—"Kissengunge batteries very quiet to-day. We have not had a shot for a couple of hours. Am very busy repairing defences, visiting the picquets, &c."

August 20*th*.—"Pretty quiet. Our spies say that the 9th N.I. have asked the King to permit them to go to their homes for a short period! The King has no objection, but won't allow them to take their arms with them, and the 60th N.I. has been *disbanded* by the King for misconduct! They were to have attacked me again yesterday, but thought better of it. They are preparing rockets for me, so writes the General. I have 101 Goorkahs sick in hospital with fever: constant work and exposure is beginning to tell on the little fellows. The enfilading fire annoys me a good deal, but the old house still stands it bravely. The walls are very thick, upwards of three feet, and all stone. The 32-pounders, however, go clean through the walls."

August 24th.—" We shall have 60 heavy guns in position on the 4th proximo. I was down with the Engineers yesterday morning looking at the proposed site for Battery No. 1. They were out surveying again this morning. The enemy did not approve, and came out to see what we were after. One of my little fellows mortally wounded; the Engineers, however, completed their survey, and returned about eight o'clock."

August 26th.—" The enemy are turning out of the city. They are going to pay me another visit apparently."

August 27th.—" The enemy thought we had sent the whole force out with Nicholson's column, so took the opportunity of once again attacking me. They found me at home, and got a good thrashing. All the ladies in the city turned out to see Hindôo Rao's House taken. They had seats erected in Kissengunge on the left of sunken batteries. The princes were present in green velvet suits covered with gold."

August 28th.—" His Majesty is coming out to-day

to see his troops take my batteries and position. I shall be very happy to see him, and only hope he will come out of the Moree Gate on the largest elephant he has got. A 24-pound shot would double up his Majesty, elephant, gold howdah, and all."

August 31*st.*—" The great Mohurrum attack came off last night. As usual they came at my poor old head. They commenced with Fort Sammy, but were driven back sharp. They gave it up as a bad business about twelve o'clock, and allowed us to go to our quarters. I am going to cut jungle to my right under their breastworks, in front of Fort Sammy. The enemy will no doubt try to prevent it—two can play at that game. I mean to drive them from their breastworks, hold them during the night, and destroy the works before we withdraw in the morning. They don't at all approve of the new trench and six-gun battery near Sammy House; when they see our 60 guns in position they will get very desperate, I doubt not."

September 1*st.*—" I drove the enemy from their breastworks last night. No sooner had I got possession, than 300 hatchets were at work felling trees, brushwood, &c. The work went on admirably the whole night in front of the trenches and Sammy House Picquet. 'Pandy' got in an awful state of mind, and we heard about a dozen bugles in the city sounding first the 'turn-out,' then the 'advance,' then the 'double;' at length the buglers got tired of the above, and sounded the 'retreat,' the only one which was obeyed. I relieved the party at eleven o'clock, when a little more popping commenced. At daybreak this morning I found a good deal had been done. I shall now be able to *see* my friends. I never knew before what force they were in when they attacked the Sammy House, so thick was the jungle on all sides. My breastworks are knocked to pieces, but I shall not have them repaired again, as we advance our batteries at once."

September 7*th.*—" We commence operations tonight. Heavy battery No. 1 will be erected during the night, and will open at daybreak ; the others will follow. No. 1 Battery is in my neighbourhood, and I have to furnish the covering-parties : not much rest for me to-night. The enemy have erected another heavy battery in ' Kissengunge,' and are annoying us a good deal. Last night we got eight light guns in position on the left of the Sammy House, but ' Reid's Battery,' as it is called, is not yet completed ; they will, I dare say, make another sortie, but I think we can drive them back. 16,000 sandbags were filled last night on Pandy land, and, to my astonishment, they did not object. I shall probably be in the trenches the whole of to-morrow."

Battery No. 1 is commanded by my dear old friend Major Brind, who has been constantly on duty with me on the Ridge, and who gave me most able assistance on the night of the Eed attack ; indeed, on all occasions the exertions of this noble officer were indefatigable. He was always to be found where his presence was most required, and the example he set to his officers and men was beyond all praise ; a finer soldier I never met.

September 9th.—" Our two heavy batteries on the right, which are protected by my picquets, in full play. The Moree replies. Two more batteries on the left will be completed to-night, one of 18 guns, the other of 6 ; the former 320 yards, the latter 160 from the city walls. My quartermaster-sergeant hit this morning and now dead. We shall be three days breaching, if not four. Cavalry and infantry sortie yesterday. No time for more. Kissengunge batteries annoy me a good deal."

" *Look-out Post,*" *September* 10*th.*—" We are hard at work with our heavy batteries on the left. They will be ready to open at daybreak to-morrow. Whilst they are getting ready on the left we are hard at work here on the right pounding the old Moree Bastion with six guns. The rascals are getting very desperate ; during the night they threw up a trench across the front of our heavy batteries, and are now firing from it, and annoying us a good deal with musketry. Their cavalry try to get up a charge, but can't quite manage it. I had a very narrow escape yesterday, and so had General Nicholson, who was standing close to me at my look-out—a shrapnel shell burst right over our heads ; three of the balls struck my telescope, which I had in my hand, but I was not touched. A Goorkah who was sitting below me lost his right eye, and another was struck in the chest. The villains will fight it out ; that I make sure of. I shall have a little work in ' Kissengunge ' ere I enter the city. I command the 4th column of attack. Have got my orders."

September 12*th*.—" We are still hard at work breaching ; the 'Moree' not yet silent, although it is almost knocked to pieces. I never saw such plucky gunners in my life. Fight it out they will, and every gunner will be killed at his gun. Poor Lockhart, doing duty with my regiment, dangerously wounded yesterday. A great loss to me. He is a first-rate officer. Every officer in the regiment killed and wounded with the exception of Fisher and myself. Hot work in the trenches. The assault will not take place before the 14th."

Notes.—About 11 A.M. on September 11, Kaye's Battery No. 2 caught fire from the constant discharge of our own guns. The sandbags first caught the flame, then the fascines, which were made of dry brushwood, and at length the whole battery was in a blaze. The enemy of course soon discovered what had happened, and they were determined that the flames should not be extinguished; they accordingly, with wonderful rapidity, brought all their heavy guns, as also every musket from the curtain walls, to bear on the blazing battery, and showers of grape were poured in. Lt. Lockhart, who was on duty with two companies of Goorkahs in the connecting trench between our batteries, Nos. 1 and 2, after consulting Major Kaye, jumped on to the parapet, followed by six or seven Goorkahs, who tried their utmost to smother the fire with sand. Two of the Goorkahs fell dead, and Lockhart rolled over the parapet with a frightful gunshot wound in the jaw, which was smashed to pieces. He lay on the

Notes—*cont.* ground some little time and then tried to jump on the parapet a second time, but at length fell from loss of blood and exhaustion. Here, indeed, was a gallant act which I witnessed myself, and a noble example set to all around and which I considered worthy of the Victoria Cross, for which I recommended Lockhart in one of my pencil reports to the General, which unfortunately, like many others written under fire at the top of Hindôo Rao's House, or behind a rock, were destroyed, as they were not considered *official*. I tried afterwards to obtain the Victoria Cross for this noble officer, but, I regret to say, did not succeed. Out of the many officers who served under me on the Delhi Ridge during the long siege which lasted three and a half months, I only recommended Lt. Minto Elliot, Bengal Artillery, and Lockhart, but neither of them received it. General Wilson had been ordered not to send in further applications for Delhi honours, and Lord Clyde, I was given to understand, considered these two officers had done nothing more than their duty.

September 12*th*, 4 P.M.—" The enemy has taken up a strong position in front of the ' Sammy House,' where they have constructed a heavy battery to enfilade our Battery No. 1. The General has ordered me to attack the position at daybreak to-morrow. There will be great loss of life, as I could not help getting under the fire of three faces of the ' Burn ' Bastion and two of the ' Moree ' Bastion. I have pointed this out to the General, and await orders."

September 12*th*, 11 p.m.—" The order countermanded."

Notes.—My column, the 4th, is composed of detachments of eight different regiments, which I object to *in toto*, as it never works well, and I have remonstrated, but fear it is too late now to alter the arrangement. I have also the Jummoo Contingent; I don't much like the look of them; I only hope they will obey orders. Captain Lawrence, my second in command, came up a short time ago, and I took him to my " look-out " and explained my plan of attack. I had General Nicholson with me early this morning. He came up to make arrangements with me regarding the assault to-morrow morning. After I had taken "Kissengunge" and cleared the enemy out of the suburbs, I proposed taking my column down the dry bed of the canal and entering the city by the Cabool Gate, which Nicholson would be able to open for me from the inside if he got there in time. I told him what an objection I had to the troops fighting in their shirt-sleeves, which they had done from the very commencement of the siege, and that I thought it had affected discipline, inasmuch as when a man turned out in his shirt-sleeves he thought he was entitled to do as he pleased. He perfectly agreed with me and said he would take very good care that the troops of his column fought in their red coats. I said I thought it would have a good effect, as the enemy had *never* seen us in red coats, and would take the "Lal Coatees " (red coats) for reinforcements which had just arrived for the assault of Delhi.

Notes—*cont.* The 60th Rifles and my own regiment on the Ridge always wore their green cloth coats, as I did myself, and we thought the cloth kept out the rays of the sun, whereas the linen sleeve was no protection, and the men's arms had a close resemblance to raw beef.

Copy of Report of the Attack of the 4th Column on the 14th September. Addressed to Major Ewart, Assistant Adjutant-General. Dated Hindóo Rao's House, 29th September, 1857.

SIR,—For the information of the Major-General commanding the forces, I have the honour to report that in obedience to instructions received I directed the troops noted in the margin (the greater portion of the Main Picquet) to form up at 4.30 A.M. on the 14th instant on the Grand Trunk Road opposite the Subzeemundee Picquet.

<small>50 H.M.'s 60th Rifles.
86 H.M.'s 61st.
70 H.M.'s 75th.
160 1st Fusiliers.
200 Sirmoor Battn.
200 Guides.
70 1st Punjaub.
65 Kumaon Battn.
Jummoo Troops.
1,200 Infantry.
400 Cavalry.
———
2,501 total strength, and 4 guns, Jummoo Contingent.</small>

Before 5 A.M. all were drawn up in perfect order, but the three Horse Artillery guns which were ordered to accompany my column had up to that time not arrived. About 5.30 they were brought up to the picquet, but the officer in charge reported that there were only gunners for one gun. I directed him to make immediate inquiries, and to get the full complement of gunners as soon as possible, as I had no intention of taking one gun into action. It was now broad daylight, and I was anxiously listening for the explosion (the blowing in of the Cashmere Gate) which was to have been my signal to advance. Nothing, however, could be heard to lead me to suppose that the assault had been made. Presently I heard musketry on my right, and soon discovered that the party of the Jummoo troops—400 infantry, 4 guns, and 200 cavalry—which I had ordered to proceed direct from camp at a quarter to 4 A.M., for the purpose of occupying the Eedghur, had become engaged with the enemy.

No time was to be lost, so I at once pushed on with the column without the Horse Artillery guns, taking the pucka road for "Kissengunge." I threw out a party of the 60th Rifles under Captain Muter, in skirmishing order on the right of the road, whilst a feeling party was sent a short distance ahead of the column.

When within sixty or seventy yards of the canal bridge, I discovered that the enemy had manned their breastwork across the road, as also one running parallel to the road, both of which had been considerably strengthened during the night. The enemy allowed me to approach within fifty yards before firing a shot, when they gave us a well-directed volley from their first breastwork.

The Rifles and Sirmoor Battalion, who were leading, I directed to charge, and the enemy were immediately driven from their strong breastwork across the road.

For some time the mutineers stood on the road, hesitating, apparently, whether they should retire on

the second breastwork, or attack the Jummoo troops
on the right. Guns at this time would have been
of the greatest service to me, and I much regret that
such a mistake should have occurred as to send guns
to me without artillerymen.

I now observed that the enemy had been reinforced
from the city, and I found myself opposed to at least
15,000 men. I was just about to make arrangements
for a feint attack in front of the Kissengunge batteries,
whilst I made a real one in flank and rear, when I
received a wound in the head, and was unable to
carry out my intentions.

I immediately sent for Captain Lawrence (who was
my second in command), to whom I had previously
given instructions, and mentioned my plan of attack
on the batteries. Whilst being carried to the rear I
met him, and directed him to take the command, and
to support the right.

Up to this time all was going on admirably, the
troops were steady and well in hand, and I made
sure of success.

I was not a little surprised to hear about an hour
after that the column had retreated, the Jummoo
troops had lost their guns, and were flying back to
camp.

All that occurred after I left the field will be
reported by Captain Lawrence.

I have the honour, &c.

CHARLES REID, *Major*,
Commanding 4th Column of Attack.

P.S.—I regret to add that my losses were very

severe, almost a third of the column. The Jummoo troops after I left the field became perfectly disorganised. They rushed into the main column, and caused the greatest confusion, when it became difficult to distinguish friend from foe.

The total loss in my own regiment, including the 14th instant, 327 killed and wounded, out of 490, all grades, and 8 officers killed and wounded out of 9.

Palace, Delhi, February 2nd, 1858.

MY DEAR ROTTON,—With regard to " Kissengunge," I can only say that, were I ordered to attack the place to-morrow, supposing the enemy's heavy guns to be in the same place they were in on the 14th September last, my plan of attack would be just what it was then.

You have been over the position, and know the localities and great strength of the place, and will, therefore, understand me when I say that by hugging the garden wall on the left of the road before you come to the canal bridge, and then the loopholed Serai wall, as also the garden wall which runs parallel to it, places one, comparatively speaking, out of harm's way. The heavy guns in the two batteries could not play, nor could the loopholes of the Serai be brought to bear, so long, mind you, as the column hugged the walls above alluded to "four deep," as I had my troops on the 14th September. The first breastwork across the road close to the canal bridge was taken, as you will see by my report, by twenty-five of the Rifles and my own regiment; but whilst making arrangements for the attack on Kissengunge itself, and the breastworks at the end of the road, I fell wounded in the head, and was thus unable, to my great disappointment, to carry out my intentions, which were as follow :—The breastworks at the end of the road I knew were very strong, as I had seen the enemy at work at them for days, and I thought it more than probable they would have light guns ready to play upon me as I advanced up the road. I therefore intended, after taking the breastwork at the canal bridge, to have made a rush with half of my column at the angle of the Serai wall, whilst the remaining half of the column (after getting rid of the enemy who had manned the garden wall, and which would have been *enfiladed*) marched parallel to the left column, and thus the breastworks at the end of the road would have been taken in *front* and *rear*. The right column would then have brought their right shoulders forward, and the columns would have entered Kissengunge *together* at the breach made in *rear* of the heavy batteries. I must here mention that some officers imagined that I had had the wall of the Serai breached in *front* of the left battery, and intended to enter there. That would have been madness indeed. The wall, 'tis true, had been pretty well breached in front of the left battery, but *bad* shots made *at* the battery had done it.

The wall *behind* the batteries was breached by my order (and right well it was done by Thompson, of

Artillery), but certainly not in *front*. Had I attempted an entrance immediately in front of the left battery, we should have been cut to pieces with grape from their two 24-pounders. No; that was quite impossible. The breaches in *rear* of the batteries, as also the gate (which I could have blown in) through which I entered on the 17th June, was my intended route into Kissengunge, whilst a *feint* attack was made in front. My object in sending 400 Infantry, 200 Cavalry, and four guns to the " Eedgha " was to make a diversion, and to place " Trevelyangunge " between a cross fire, as also to watch the enemy, and prevent our right flank being turned.

After getting possession of " Kissengunge," I should have turned the four heavy captured guns, as also the two 8-inch mortars which they had there, on " Trevelyangunge." The fire from these guns (as also from the guns which I *ought* to have had with me), and the fire which would have been kept up by the four guns from the " Eedgha," would have made " Trevelyangunge " too hot for the enemy, and I calculated on their retreating into the city.

Certain it is, I should not have attempted to have turned them out of Trevelyangunge and Pahareepore with my infantry. My column was not strong enough for that, and I should have lost half of my men before I entered the city. Had the enemy left Trevelyangunge, which I think they would have done when they found themselves under the fire of artillery from Kissengunge and the Eedgha, I should have left 400 of the Jummoo Contingent in the Serai, whilst I proceeded with the rest of the column along the dry bed of the canal, and have entered the city at the Cabool Gate, which General Nicholson would have opened for me from the inside.

This was my intended attack on "Kissengunge." A good deal would, of course, have depended on circumstances; but certain it is, I should not have entered the city so long as the enemy were in force on my right.

Some say, "Why not have gone more to the right, and have given 'Kissengunge' a wider berth?" Had I done so the enemy would have got in between my left flank and the "Subzee-mundee," which our spies told us they intended to do. Others again say, "Why not have taken the same route you took on the 17th of June, when you succeeded in taking the place?" To which I reply, for the same reasons I have given above—my flank would have been turned.

In conclusion, I must mention that it was my desire that "Kissengunge" should have been attacked before daybreak; but it was decided that all should attack at the same time, and that my signal to advance was to be the explosion—the blowing in of the "Cashmere Gate." This did not take place until a quarter of an hour after sunrise, by which time, of course, the enemy were on the alert, and quite ready for us in "Kissengunge."

You are at liberty to publish the whole of the above *verbatim*. Yours sincerely,
CHARLES REID.

Rev. J. Rotton, Chaplain, Delhi Field Force.

"Kissengunge" was evacuated by the enemy on the morning of the 16th, all their heavy guns and mortars being left in the batteries. A party was sent from Hindôo Rao's House to take possession of them, and they were brought up safely to the Ridge. The immense strength of the position astonished all who afterwards inspected it. I was unable to go over the place myself till the end of November, not having sufficiently recovered from the effects of my wound. As may be imagined, I went over the Serai of Kissengunge, which I had taken on the 17th June, with the greatest interest. The insurgents had certainly spared no labour to improve what was then even immensely strong; from the 6th of August they had been daily employed in erecting breastworks, batteries, &c.; Trevelyangunge and Pahareepore were also considerably strengthened, and the wonder is the enemy left the position without another struggle. The bullet marks on the canal bridge, the Serai wall, and garden walls showed pretty clearly what showers had been sent at my column, and the only wonder is our loss was not even greater than it really was.

I will not attempt to describe my feelings as I strolled over my old position on the Ridge. When I looked at the ground round about Hindôo Rao's House—ploughed up with shot and shell, the rocks split and covered with bullet-marks, trees cut in two and branches torn, and the old house itself riddled through and through with shot and shell, fragments of which still lay upon the ground although cartloads had been removed—it appeared, I may say, a miracle that I stood there gazing upon the scene. When I looked at particular places in the "Subzeemundee," where I had seen my troops on the 23rd June driving the enemy before them, and again retreating under a burning sun, a deadly fire of artillery and of musketry, and a vastly superior force, I exclaimed, Can it be—is it possible—am I really a living being after all I have gone through?

Of the strength of Delhi itself I need not speak; but it did not consist in its actual defences only, though these were very much undervalued; the Moree, Cashmere, and Burn Bastions had been greatly improved by our own Engineers (Baird Smith amongst them), some years before, and presented regular faces with properly cut embrasures. The length of the wall was twenty-four feet above ground level, eight feet of which was a parapet three feet thick, the remainder being about four times that thickness; outside the walls was a wide berm, and a ditch eighteen feet deep and twenty feet wide at bottom. The glacis covered the lower ten feet of the wall, and the curtain walls connecting the bastions were loopholed. Added to these strong defences, it must be remembered that the enemy possessed a magazine containing upwards of two hundred guns, and sufficient ammunition for half-a-dozen sieges, while their numbers of trained troops and excellent gunners were certainly three, if not four, times the strength of the besiegers. But all this has been already written, so I need not dwell upon it; but suffice it to say that the contemplated *coup-de-main*, first in June and afterwards in July, would, in all human probability, have proved a signal failure.

I cannot conclude without alluding to the noble behaviour of the officers and men of the Bengal Artillery, who served under me on the Delhi Ridge. I more than once made mention of their gallant conduct in my daily pencil reports; but, as I have before stated, these were never published, which I cannot but regret. There can be no brighter passage in the history of the Delhi siege than that which will tell of their trials and exertions before Delhi.

The engineer officers' duties were most laborious, and they were much exposed. The Delhi siege was, indeed, a good school for our young engineers, and it certainly brought out their abilities; they were constantly exposed to a burning sun and a deadly fire, as their losses clearly showed, being nearly two-thirds in killed and wounded.

It would be impossible to speak too highly of Colonel Baird Smith and Major Taylor; from them I received every assistance; they were ever ready to meet my wishes, and every effort was used by them to strengthen our position on the Ridge. For our ultimate success we have to thank these two men. Owing to a wound received by Colonel Baird Smith, the entire superintendence of the siege operations devolved on Taylor, and a more energetic officer I never met; the rapidity with which he completed No. 1 battery on the night of the 7th of September was perfectly surprising; no one was more taken aback than " Pandy " himself when the day dawned and he beheld six 24-pounders within 600 yards of him.

Although these notes are not now intended for publication I cannot close them without expressing my heartfelt gratitude to all (officers and men) who served under me from first to last. Their courage and endurance, and their cheerful obedience to all orders they received, won my esteem, and I have to thank them for the high honour I have received from Her Most Gracious Majesty. Without such men I never could have held the position entrusted to me.

www.ingramcontent.com/pod-product-compliance
Lightning Source LLC
Chambersburg PA
CBHW032007080426
42735CB00007B/536